Time Well Spent

TERI MILLER

TIME WELL SPENT

3 Generations, 2 Sons-in-law, 2 ½ Babies, a Puppy, Covid & Jesus

COPYRIGHT © 2022 BY TERI MILLER

All rights reserved. No part of this publication may be reproduced, stored in a retrieval system or transmitted in any form or by any means, electronic, mechanical, photocopying, recording or otherwise without the prior permission of the publisher. Short extracts may be used for review purposes.

Unless other wised noted all scripture are taken from the Holy Bible, New Living Translation *(NLT)*, copyright c 1996, 2004,2007,2013,2015 by Tyndale House Foundation. Used by permission of Tyndale House Publishers, Inc., Carol Stream, Illinois 60188. All rights reserved.

ISBN: 979-8-9859114-1-1

DESIGN:	CARLI JEEN RICHARDS
HEADSHOT:	CARLI JEEN RICHARDS
BACK COVER PHOTO:	RACHEL ALBRECHT
COVER PAINTING:	TAMI KING
TITLE SUGGESTION:	ANDREA RICHARDS
	(thanks Andrea)

Printed in the USA

FORWARD

BY

Joyelle Lee

COFOUNDER OF BARN45
BARN45.ORG

"CHECK YOUR SHAME AT THE DOOR, IT AIN'T WELCOME ANYMORE."

The Fathers House by Cory Asbury

I envision this as our theme song as it delicately dances through Teri's home speakers as we're drawn to step into her inviting book, smelling of deliciously baked chocolate chip cookies, an atmosphere of just the right amount of rawness and a steaming cup of freshly brewed coffee, made just to your liking, in your favorite Joanna Gaines mug.

I can imagine you're now humming along with me secretly wondering if the lyrics you're singing could ever reflect the reality you're living?

And you may even be wondering if a book entitled,

"*Time Well Spent*," is truly a way to spend your time well, because ultimately, as J.R.R. Tolkien once said, "All we have to decide is what to do with the time that is given us."

Well, dear friend, sink down, relax, exhale and dare to accept the invitation into Teri's home on the lake. Because it's here you'll be met with her warm smile that reaches to her ears, all while reaching straight to your heart. You'll be introduced to her husband's integrity, her children's humor and her grandsons' contagious giggles.

Above all else, I promise you, you can trust your heart to her as she gently places your hand into hers, leading you to the back door view of her calm and still lake -- a sweet reminder of the One who says, "I will fight for you, you need only to be still." ~ Exodus 14:14.

Teri's epistolary style of writing is drenched with authenticity, practicality, relatability and applicability while also being seasoned with a perfectly measured dash of humor, wisdom and the promises of our faithful God. As her book quotes, these pages contain moments, days, seasons of "Both hard and good all at the same time."

"*Time Well Spent*" is Teri's invitation for you to come as you are, pull up a well-loved kitchen chair and spend an afternoon gleaning from both the richness and kindness of her Jesus found in the everyday life of the Miller family.

From Covid to cookies. Babies to barbecues. Heartaches to belly laughs. Tears to repairs. Each page reveals the character of a restorative God who revealed Himself to be unshakably faithful in a season of three generations, two sons-in-law, two-and-a-half babies, a puppy, a pandemic and Jesus all under one perfectly, imperfect roof.

The title of Teri's book whispers what your heart will declare as you turn over the final page... this was indeed, *"Time Well Spent."*

TIME WELL SPENT

PERSPECTIVE
FOR THE READER

Hindsight is 2020. As you read about some of the situations we were confronted with during the past couple of years, please remember that we now live with the benefit of time and experience.

Time Well Spent includes my thoughts, challenges and views regarding what was happening, as it was happening. I have not altered anything as I have gone through and reviewed the content. My perspective and opinions have changed on several issues, and that's okay. As time passes, information becomes available and our views on certain issues are modified.

This is not intended to be a political book. It is a book about heart, family and the experience of living during tumultuous times.

TIME WELL SPENT

YEAR 2020

June	28
July	32
August	46
September	68
October	82
November	100
December	110

YEAR 2021

January	128
February	146
March	160
April	176
May	194
June	204
July	218
August	230

DEDICATION

I always think I'll remember the important events in my life. Then time passes, and I am so grateful for the pictures that were taken because I realize how much I forget.

This book is a love letter to my family and myself because I didn't want any of us to forget a moment of our time together. I dedicate this memoir to my generous and loving husband and children. They have allowed me to share their personal stories without hesitation or edits. They are brave, honest, and my biggest inspiration.

In recent years, writing has really become a passion of mine. And the moment my husband and I discovered all of our adult children, their spouses, and their children were moving back in with us, I was moved to document our journey. As it happened, it was also a great outlet for my processing, as life was happening on a grand scale. Writing throughout our time together has made room for God to speak His truth and His enough-love to my heart as He always does when I sit down at my keyboard or with a pen and a notebook.

We write because through writing we discover truth that we didn't know we knew. We write because one of the ways God speaks to us is through our stories."
- Dan Allender

SETTING THE STAGE

We were daydreaming. It was a perfect, sunny, fall day in Michigan. The leaves were beginning to burst with bright oranges, reds, and yellows. My husband, Michael, and I borrowed our neighbor's pontoon boat, and it was the first time we'd taken it out alone. It's nice to have neighbors who are friends but feel more like family, and John and Lisa kept their beautiful new boat docked on a lake inside of a metro park near our home. This particular lake is surrounded by trees and picturesque picnic areas, making it unusually peaceful and quiet, not at all like the rest of the lakes near our home. Most lakes in Michigan are surrounded by homes, one after another, so close together you can practically pass the salt from one patio to another. They are filled with people and parties and laughter and all of the water toys that accompany a lake lifestyle, but for us on that magical day, the lake we were on was quiet and peaceful. The sun was shining, the breeze was blowing, and hot air balloons were painting the sky. The only sounds we heard were the music coming from our playlist and our quiet conversation. It was a perfect day to dream.

My husband Mike and I are at the age where retirement is beginning to creep into our conversations every once in a while. We know it's more than a few years away, but with how fast time is flying, it will be here before we know it. And we don't want our future to catch us unprepared. We want to remain active, and we desire to stay engaged with family, friends, and ministry, whatever that may look like. Moving forward, we want to be even more prayerful, deliberate, and present with this next season of our life together. Getting older, having grandkids, watching our parents age, and seeing the world the way it is has made us evaluate our priorities and the legacy we will someday leave behind more than we ever have before. These are weighty topics to contemplate, but we've learned the value of intention, and we want to steer the boat, so to speak, as much as possible in this next chapter, to avoid getting pushed by every circumstantial wind that might come our way. We agreed on that beautiful day on the boat that the desire of our heart for the next season of our life would focus on our children, grandchildren, and the people God puts in our path to love on. We also agreed that in the best-case scenario, we would prefer to do this living in a home on the water, preferably surrounded by lots of trees, birds, and beautiful sunrises or sunsets. As we talked on the boat that day, we dreamed out loud about how special and fun it would be to live in a private and quiet place, with space to enjoy the people God puts in our path.

Like I said, we were just daydreaming as all of those things are very difficult to find in our price range in Michigan. We also discussed the possibility of moving south if necessary. However, we agreed that we didn't want to move away from the life we knew and the people we loved just to live on the water, so that was not an option without a direct word from the Lord. As the sun began to set, we asked God to guide our steps and lead us into this next season. We left the lake that day with color in our cheeks and a dream growing in our hearts.

We felt prompted to not wait until we retired to put our feelers out for this possible new adventure. Carpe Diem right? Who knows what tomorrow holds?

"Let's just see what's out there," we said.

As a result of our day on the water, I also began feeling a divine push to sell our present home, so I began cleaning and staging just in case. I also assigned my two adult daughters, Carli and Mallory, and my friend Shelley who is a realtor, the task of discovering what homes were available in our area.

Very quickly, I began receiving listings of houses that were typical for our area—nice homes on beautiful lakes—but none of them were what my heart desired. Then one day, Carli, who lived in California at the time, found a lakefront property listed on Zillow not too far outside the local boundary we were currently considering. It had 1.6 acres, 4 bedrooms, 3 full baths, and a large walkout basement just begging to be finished. And the price was right. The value was substantially diminished because it had been neglected for almost twenty years. I think the amount of work it would take to bring it back to life scared everyone else away, so it had been on the market for over a year, just waiting for us.

It was a hidden gem though because it sat on a lake partially surrounded by a community park. This lake was very similar to the one we were on when we were daring to dream that day on the boat. At the time, I didn't even know there was a lake that shared a park and homes. Neither did my realtor or my friends, but God did. I am so aware of His hand in all of this.

There is one other time in my life when I felt like God literally picked me up from one place and plopped me down in another. That time was almost eight years ago. In that circumstance, He knew what I needed, and He knew I didn't have the strength to get there on my own. He used people and circumstances, painful ones unfortunately, to move me to a healthier, better place — a place He had waiting for me. It wasn't until a few years later, after much healing, that I was able to fully recognize His hand in all of it and the grace that I and my whole family were covered in. Finding this new house was similar to that experience in that God knew what I wanted and needed even more than I did. This time; however, I was in a happier, healthier place and His divine push was all I needed to get there.

We purchased our home on Independence Lake in December 2019, and we sold the home we were living in a few months later. We accepted an offer in February and then waited for all of the paperwork, inspections, etc. to proceed to our closing. This meant we were going to own two homes for a short period of time. Not an ideal situation, but it worked out best for us at the time because of all of the renovations that needed to be made to our lakefront property. It was a seller's market, and we were living on a very desirable street in a really cute little town. We felt the risk was low, and we had peace about it. So that's what we did.

Meanwhile, a highly contagious, unprecedented virus was making its way across the world. We watched as the news revealed what was happening in China. People were rioting in the streets of Hong Kong to fight for democracy, and then the streets were empty. No more riots. No more people. It was bazaar and kind of scary, but it was happening in China, so none of us were too worried because it was on the other side of the world.

Then we watched Italy shut down. Pictures of empty streets and talk of this potentially deadly and unknown virus were like something out of a movie. Countries were closing borders. Businesses were closing their doors. Cities were abandoned. It was scary.

Then it was here. In America. What once was only on the news began to affect our lives.

If you can, think back to how uncertain everything was. We had never experienced a shutdown where everything was closed for weeks and in some circumstances closed for months, causing the streets to become empty. It was very surreal, and for me, it felt like I was living in a scene from *World War Z* or *I am Legend*.

The contrasting realities we were all experiencing were unique, to say the least. One reality was the unusual experience of being confined to our homes — sometimes enjoying the down time, cleaning closets, getting crafty and reading books we've been wanting to read while at other times and often simultaneously living another reality. One with loneliness, sickness and even death. It was a frightening and very difficult time, prompting anxiety and stress at unprecedented levels. For many of us, these realities collided, as it seemed none of us were exempt from a portion of either of these realities — conversations about pajama pants and Zoom calls, job loss and fear of the unknown. I couldn't help but marvel at the unusual juxtaposition of it all. And, while all of this was beginning to happen, we now owned two homes. Yippie! (I say tongue in cheek.) How could God let this happen? We had prayed, and we were trusting God. Now here we were in this seemingly highly unfortunate situation with no guide to tell us how to navigate this scary and unpredictable future we were facing. Or was there?

While the world, literally the whole world, was figuring all of this out, we had to figure out what this meant for us and our current situation. No way could we afford two homes. The sale of our house had to go through, but common sense or possibly fear told us no one was going to spend the amount we were counting on during this uncertain time. No way. So we did what we always do. We took turns reminding each other what the Word of God says, as the Bible is our guide to life.

I know I said this season was unprecedented, so how could the Bible tell us what to do about living in a world with Covid-19 and during an election year too? As you may very well know, the Word of God can always guide us. Even in the most unusual of times.

I heard the Spirit whisper, "Peace, be still".

My husband heard God say to his spirit, "Do you trust me?"

He answered, in his heart and mind, "Yes, I trust You."

We've lived long enough with the Lord to know that "He will never leave us or forsake us" (Deuteronomy 31:6). If we "cast our cares on Him, He will care for us" (1 Peter 5:7), for we know how much "He loves us" (John 3:16). We reminded each other to "seek the kingdom of God" (Matthew 6:33), to "yield to His will" (Proverbs 3:5-6), and to "listen for His voice" (John 10:27), for we can always trust Him. We only needed to continue to "place our hope and trust in Him" (Jeremiah 29:11).

Now, don't get me wrong, I'm not saying that there weren't any negative feelings that accompanied this crazy journey. We did experience fear. We did feel worried and stressed at times, but we continued to remind ourselves of the truth we hold dear. We prayed, a lot. Once again, we found ourselves desperate for God to move, and I know that when I'm desperate and relying on God, it's about to get good.

Two days before our closing at the end of March, you guessed it—our buyers walked. We got a call from our realtor Shelley with the devastating news that our buyers were forfeiting their deposit and pulling out of our deal. I remember where I was when we got that call. It was around nine o'clock at night, and Mike and I were doing what we were usually doing those evenings, painting at the new house. Every inch of every wall and ceiling and all of the wood trim needed at least three coats of paint. As you can imagine, it was a very satisfying but also exhausting project. While other people were home cooking and binging on Netflix, we were over at the other house painting and cleaning. That night, we were surprised to hear from her, in the evening, just days away from our closing. We sat on the stairs near the living room listening to her struggle to speak on the other side of the phone. She was in tears because she had tried to talk the buyers out of it, and it didn't go well. She was frightened for us and heartbroken as she gave us the news that the deal fell through. We were going to have to start all over again. In March. In the middle of a dreary Michigan winter. During Covid. Not ideal.

There are divine moments in life when your spirit-man flexes its muscle and reminds your soul that God is in control. This was one of those moments for me. It had honestly never occurred to me that they would back out. Naively, I assumed when someone made an agreement with you and actually put money on the line to show they were serious (and it's two days away from closing), they were committed. As I listened to Mike and Shelley talk about what recourse we could take, I had a peace that welled up on the inside, and I told them I knew it was going to be okay. Mike was also calm and agreed. He told Shelley that God had taken us to this place and He wouldn't leave us now. The scriptures that immediately ran through my mind during that phone call were Proverbs 15:15, "A gentle answer deflects anger, but harsh words make tempers flare," and Romans 12:18, "Do all that you can to live in peace with everyone." I knew that trying to work it out with the buyers was the direction we were to pursue.

It may sound like I'm bragging, but trust me I'm not. It was totally the Holy Spirit within me that gave me peace in that moment. It was the grace of God that was covering us. We were both very much aware of it. I knew what I needed to do. I just knew, like another divine push, to reach out to the buyers and connect with them. I have come to understand this is not typically done, but we had nothing to lose. I sat down in the quiet and dark of my half-painted living room. Sherwin Williams Snowbound white satin coated my hair and my hands, and I wrote an e-mail to our buyers telling them we understood their fear of moving during a pandemic and lockdown and asked them to consider talking with us about their decision. Surprisingly, they agreed.

I talked with the couple on the phone the following night. I felt in my spirit they were simply afraid as February and March were very uncertain and scary, to say the least. Somehow I just knew if I was able to speak to them and reason with them peacefully, they would change their minds. Miraculously they did, and we saw them a few days later at our curbside closing. It was another first for us. We pulled up to the mortgage company and signed papers in our car. And just like that, it was done, and we were the proud owners of one home again. Praise God!

Side note, this incident started a text relationship between the wife and me. She thanked me for being "so nice" about it all. See, a soft answer really does turn away wrath. She communicated to me that they thought the phone call was going to be full of anger and rage, and when it wasn't, they were caught off guard and motivated to change their minds. The lovely thing is we've been able to answer questions for them about the house, and she's called me to come get mail that didn't get transferred to our new home. It's pretty cool how when you actually live with the Word of God as your guide, peace can invade a world filled with chaos.

I give all of this information as context for the rest of this book, journal, devotional, compilation of entries — whatever this book turns out to be. This home was a divine appointment, not only for Mike and me but for our children as well. It opened up the possibility for us all to isolate together.

Our son, the youngest of the three, had recently returned from college and was currently living with us. He was excited about living for a little while on a lake surrounded by nature. After we purchased this new home with a potential apartment in the basement, my middle child, Mallory, asked if she and her husband and their precious little son Silas could move into our basement once it was completed to help them pay off student loans and save for a larger house. We said "yes" without hesitation and were delighted at the prospect of being able to spend a season living with their precious little family.

While we were renovating the house, taking down walls, adding windows, and working on finishing the basement, my oldest daughter, Carli, was dealing with the sqeeze of looming shutdowns. In her spontaneous nature and desire to lock down together, she canceled her scheduled wedding date and got married to her handsome fiancé in a very intimate wedding with just immediate family.

Carli and Cole were the last couple to receive a wedding license in San Diego before California totally shut down. Having no idea how long this pandemic would last and being very much in love, they decided to get married within the week. They made this decision on a Monday, and we were on an eerily empty plane headed to Cali on Thursday for the blessed event. It really was a blessed event. It was a beautiful, anointed, lovely time with just our immediate families. It was not like any wedding we had ever been to. We shared the wedding on Facebook Live, and I'm pretty sure it was one of the first weddings experienced this way during the pandemic. They were married in an almost empty church, had the reception in the parking lot of an In-and-Out Burger, and took pictures on the beach at Torrey Pines next to the Pacific Ocean. It was unique and special, just like our Carli.

After weeks of California being completely shut down, it became apparent that my new son-in-law's chimney sweeping business was greatly affected by the lack of business. Rather than try to find something totally new during this difficult time, they decided to continue on their unique journey and make the move to Michigan to be with us for a while.

As 2020 would have it, their cross-country honeymoon was during the tragic death of George Floyd, which sparked riots in the streets all across the country. As this precious couple tried to make their way from the West Coast to the Midwest, towing everything they owned behind them in a U-Haul, they were forced to avoid cities that were literally burning down. They did finally make it safely to us, along with a new puppy they picked up in Colorado and a fresh "bun in the oven". Surprise!

I wrote this memoir from my still-being-renovated home, with our three adult children, two sons-in-law, a precious grandson, a new puppy named Pepper, and a precious little one we had yet to meet. These are the stories chronicling the journey of our lives together as we hunkered down during 2020 and some of 2021. The most unique and troubling years in our country's history, at least while I've been alive.

God brought us all together for a reason. I'm not sure exactly what it is yet, but I trust Him. I know He has a plan and purpose for each one of us, and He is always working things together for our good.

Our time together was a crazy ride full of ups and downs. I knew I would need to write about it, not only for my sanity but also for my joy.

I don't know if we'll ever fully understand what God was up to when He reunited us all in the big house on the lake. But I can say with confidence that we grew a little bit closer, and each one of us had an abundance of support and camaraderie during a very difficult season. We did have our share of struggles, arguments, and tears; but we also had an abundance of intimate, loving conversations, great times relaxing and playing together, and much laughter and joy. The memories are precious and many.

SETTING THE STAGE

AS YOU READ, IT IS MY INTENTION
THAT YOU TOO WILL ENJOY THE
JOURNEY AND AGREE,
IT WAS DEFINITELY...

Time Well Spent

June

2020
ENTRY ONE

Carli and Cole moved in a few days ago, along with their new puppy Pepper. It's so good to have them here. They are working to make their room a little oasis with new reading lamps and matching green antique reading chairs. There's a cow skin rug, brass mirrors, and all kinds of yummy pillows and bedding, perfect for making the room cozy and inviting. They are next door to Nicholas, who gave up the biggest room for the one next door. He is at the end of the hall and has made his space inviting as well. An American flag and a Michigan Wolverines throw cover his walls, and the Papasan chair I got when we were newlyweds over thirty-five years ago is the perfect seat for playing video games.

I suspect we will all need our own special places where we can go to get away from the noise and busyness of a house full of people. My sanctuary is our bedroom with plenty of space for my office. My desk rests against a large window overlooking the backyard and the lake. It's a view I never dreamed I would see every day. Our home faces east, so every morning we see a breathtaking sunrise on display. Even on the days when it is rainy or cold, the lake view never disappoints.

Fresh beginnings are exciting, but they can also be a little scary. As we approach this time together, I think we are all realistic about how extraordinarily unique this opportunity is. We are under no illusions that it will be all campfires and laughter. There will be times of struggle as well. But that's life, isn't it? Ups and downs. Mountains and valleys. No one's life is perfect. Even Jesus found himself crying in the garden of Gethemane, struggling with His reality of facing death on a cross. I'm just glad to know that He is with us on this journey, for however long it lasts. We know that He is with us. Loving us and growing and stretching us and hopefully making each one of us more like Himself.

ENTRY TWO

The days go by so fast. Today I started my day on the porch. Coffee, Bible, journal, and the beautiful sunrise over the water. I read in Psalms, and the writer told me that gratitude honors God. I have much to be thankful for, but today I didn't express my gratitude for the people, places, and things in my life, even though I am overflowing with joy for many, many things. Today I spent some time telling God how grateful I am that He drew me to Himself by His Spirit. I am grateful that He has placed His Spirit within me so that I can experience His Presence and His great love. I expressed my love to Him and spent some time enjoying our quiet conversation.

After breakfast, I headed to our almost finished basement for a day of painting. The painting seems endless on this home improvement, DIY, fixer upper. This week's project is painting the kitchen cabinets we salvaged from the upstairs kitchen. As with the rest of the basement, we're going with mostly white. I love the color white. White clothes, white car, white yeti, white walls. Some might say it looks clinical, but I think it's going to be a fresh, inviting place for my daughter Mallory, her husband Jacob, and their little man Silas. They recently sold their home and should be moving in around the end of the month. It's going to be a full house. I'm excited for all of the voices and life that is going to happen here.

As I sit at my desk to write, it's almost 9:30 at night, and I'm still in my paint clothes. I see Carli and Cole down by the water with their new little puppy, Pepper. Cole is attempting to catch one of the decent size fish that we all believe is in our lake but has yet to bite, and Carli is reading her book and watching her new husband. Even though I am tired from painting all day, I am content; and honestly, feeling tired feels good. I feel like I've been inactive the past few years. It feels good to know that I actually made a huge impact on the kitchen downstairs today. I'm happy knowing that Mallory and her sweet family will be putting their plates, cups, and bowls down there soon.

Very soon

July

2021
ENTRY ONE

Feeling the squeeze of transition today. Sunday, the last of our kids moved in. Mallory, Jacob, and baby Silas joined the party. Unfortunately, the basement suite isn't completely done, so it's a partial move-in with clothes on the floor and pantry food on the counter. This is a challenge with a little one and two working parents. We are going to finish the closets and pantry this week, but it is a work in progress. We are all definitely feeling the emotions of extreme change.

Change is a funny thing. Even when it's for the better, it doesn't necessarily make it any easier. We learn and grow, and that ultimately brings new levels of maturity into our lives. New school. New job. New friends. You get the idea.

But just because we know it's going to be better for us in the long run or just the next stage in life, doesn't mean it doesn't hurt. My oldest, Carli, is four months pregnant, and she is experiencing pain in her back and hips. This discomfort is caused by her body making room for the baby girl to grow inside of her. It's necessary but definitely not enjoyable.

Sometimes, change is really hard. Personally, I'm not a big fan of change. I'm one of those people who put my furniture in one place when I move in and rarely change it. Pictures hang on my walls for years. I once had a clock on my wall that I got as a wedding gift, and Carli came home from school and pointed out that, "Maybe I could find something a little nicer to go there." And she was right. I had become house blind to it. But once it had been pointed out to me, I was irritated by it every time I looked at it. It was old and outdated, and I finally became ready for a change, but it still took me a while to warm up to the idea. Sometimes I envy people who love to move or redecorate or change their hairstyles without much thought. I wish I were more that way, but the part of me that is steady and consistent and trustworthy is also the part of me that can limit what I do or where I go. If I'm not open to the Spirit of God leading my life, my strengths can also become my weaknesses, and I can resist the change that will benefit me in the end.

Because of God's goodness, He often prepares my heart for the change He is about to bring in my life. As I pray and surrender my life to Him daily, He will prepare me for what's coming next. Often, He creates a want to or a divine push for me to do something new, much like I mentioned in the introduction of this book. Some people hear an audible voice or hear a voice in their spirits they recognize as not their own, while others get an illuminated Word as they read the Bible. I have experienced all of these forms of hearing from God, but the divine push and the new desire or want to are how I experience His moving in my life the most. Like the desire to make a CD, write a book, send a card of encouragement, or get an education at the age of fifty, enabling me to become a counselor. All are examples of God's divine push in my life. Most recently, the push included us living on a lake... with all three of our kids, their spouses, a new puppy, a ten-month-old, and a baby on the way... you get the idea.

JULY 2020

ENTRY TWO

Yesterday was exactly the kind of day I anticipated having after we bought this house and learned that all the kids were coming home. During the past months, as Mike and I worked to make this messy old house a shiny new home, I would look out the windows and daydream about what life might look like with all of us here. As I painted, I prayed for the lives that would dwell within these freshly painted walls. As I cleaned and worked and made design choices, I would look out the window and dream of us in the yard together, enjoying the summer sun. But often, what we imagine isn't what we experience, so as the day turned to night and what I had hoped for was actually happening, I was filled with a contentment that only comes from being surrounded by the people you love.

I knew there would be collaborative dinners made in our new kitchen or informal dinners eaten with conversations flowing, with the backdrop of a baby in his highchair wanting food quicker than his momma and daddy could shovel in. That is exactly what we had today. I had hoped we'd be by the water in the evenings, and last night there was quiet reflection and underlying competition as the guys continued to break in their new Father's Day fishing poles. Excitement broke the tranquility as Mallory, who had borrowed her hubby's fishing pole, caught her first fish. She caught the only fish of the evening. One for the girls.

After dinner and fishing, we sat around the fire and talked about the issues that weighed heavily on our hearts. Violence in our country. A virus that is affecting and isolating people to a degree none of us ever imagined. The role of social media in our lives. Our differing ages, temperaments, and upbringings made for deep and meaningful conversations. We didn't always agree or see things through identical lenses, but there was a mutual quest for truth and peace, and it was beautiful.

As evening moved to night, we moved closer and closer to the fire until it was clear the cool air and mosquitos had won and it was time to call it a night.

One thing was missing tonight though, my son, Nic. He is working and I miss him. His work schedule keeps him away a lot in the evenings, and I fear that his physical absence could contribute to his feeling left out. This weighs on my heart and infiltrates my prayers as I sit at my desk and write.

I'm very aware of our need to belong. I've heard it said that people grow where they are accepted.

I've experienced this in my life. Something as simple as an acknowledgment, a greeting, or a look of understanding can heal a soul. It's deep within us, the need to be seen. We hunger to be known and accepted. And satan, the thief, the great liar, comes to us at our youngest age and whispers lies to us about who we are and what we are not. His greatest goal is for us to believe we don't belong, that we are not loved or cherished. He delights when we feel damaged or ashamed. These beliefs keep us from opening up and allowing others to really see us. If you feel this way as you read my words—separated, alone, not good enough—this is not God's will for your life! Would you pause and ask God to show you where these beliefs came from? Perhaps on a playground or in a lunchroom many years ago. In your home or at your job?

What moment comes to mind? What are the words that echo in your head that sound a lot like your own? If they keep you from allowing others to really see you, they are from the enemy of your soul, the devil.

God wants to change the story. Trust me, we all have those painful memories where we were humiliated, embarrassed, bullied, or even abused; and the devil wants us to think we're the only one. You're not the only one. May I encourage you to allow God to speak truth to you today. May you understand as you read my words that God loves you and accepts you just the way you are. He created you, quirks and all, and He understands your pain. He is not angry with you or ashamed of you. He is pouring out His love on you today. May you have the courage and vulnerability to receive it!

Who knows, you might find yourself huddled around a campfire with precious people, accepted and loved, and the joy it brings you may surprise you.

ENTRY THREE

"My cup runneth over." I just finished watching *Hope Floats* with Sandra Bullock and Harry Connick Jr. I cry every time I watch it, yet when it's on or I see it On Demand, I have a hard time resisting it. Even though the story takes you through the hardest season of Birdee's (Sandra's character) life, you see the beauty in the journey and the love shared in the pain as you watch the story progress. I guess that's why I love the story so much. It truly is a dose of hope and a reminder that even during the most difficult seasons of our lives, if we will continue on and press through there is good waiting for us on the other side. It is also a touching story about the love and pain between a mother and her daughter, and how it impacts their lives. It's a beautiful expression of the messy, not perfect, love that we share in our families. During a tender moment with her granddaughter, Birdee's mother shares that because of the love that they share, her cup runneth over (stated this way in the King James Version of the Bible). Meaning, she is blessed beyond measure. At the end of the movie, after much heartache and pain, the granddaughter shares the same sentiment with her mother, Birdee. A full circle moment. As I watch with tears resting on my cheeks and my throat squeezed tight, I agree. My cup also runs over with the love and goodness of God expressed in those I love the most.

The line, "My cup runs over, or overflows with blessings," is taken from Psalm 23:5. It says, "The Lord is my Shepherd; I have all I need..." Verse 23:5 says, "You prepare a feast for me in the presence of my enemies. You honor me by anointing my head with oil. My cup overflows with blessings."

David was able to write these words while he had real enemies who wanted to destroy him. In the midst of the trial, while he was navigating the joys, trials and sorrows of his life, he experienced the anointing, provision, and love of God. It didn't matter if he was in a deep valley or rejoicing over a great victory, these truths were his constant companion. I am jealous for this kind of relationship with God. I want to know Him, trust Him, rely on Him, and recognize His hand in my life like David did. It is my constant prayer, that I would know Him more.

Seeking perspective

ENTRY FOUR

I came downstairs from my bedroom this afternoon, and the living room and kitchen were a mess. Shoes everywhere, pillows on the floor next to the baby and dog toys, and the island, that I'm a little overly nutty about keeping clean, was covered with laptops, used glasses of water and pop, and an old plate of nachos. You get the idea. I was surprised by my response at the sight. I'll be honest, there have been times recently when I dread the mess. I have gotten frustrated when people don't clean up after themselves. It is a challenge for me to communicate with my "kids" about how we are each responsible for our own messes, and if we are truly going to live in peace, we need to all be willing to clean up after ourselves and each other once in a while. But this moment wasn't that. I just stood there and enjoyed the view, surrounded by the reality that we were all here together.

How crazy is it that God took us from our 1,600 square foot ranch with a driveway that could only hold two cars at a time and brought us to this huge four-bedroom home with a full apartment in the basement and a driveway and yard that easily holds the six cars that all of us currently drive, with room for friends and family. It's still a crazy mystery to me what God is up to. I know when we look back in a year or so, we will see what He wanted to accomplish in our lives, but now while we're living it, I can't help but wonder.

Selling our cute little forever home and moving into a house on a lake was definitely a surprise. We were fine, comfortably living our very quiet lives on the cul-de-sac. Then we were no longer fine. We were divinely discontented. The prospect of positioning ourselves to love and serve people better was becoming our heart's desire. We had no idea at the time that our children would be the first recipients. We had no idea that a global pandemic was going to strike and change life as we knew it. But God knew. As I think about the peace I feel today as I gaze upon the shoes and dirt and stuff all around, I realize that this is what you get when you love and serve people–a beautiful mess.

ENTRY FIVE

When living with seven adults, a ten-month-old, and a puppy, there are a lot of feelings happening in our house at any given moment. We are all dealing with life, managing Covid-19 with all of its frustrations and limitations. Some of us are navigating a recent move across the country as newlyweds, while others are moving into a basement, while it's still being completed, with a little one. Several of us are working in new jobs, while others have quit jobs and are currently interviewing for new ones. And during all of this, we are preparing for and planning a wedding reception that didn't get to happen because of Covid. As a result of all of this living, it's a constant feeling-fest, both positive and negative. While we are supporting one another and are all very glad we get to have this amazing time together, I am personally processing all of the feelings that are taking place in my home.

I could not have lived with my adult children and their children five years ago. It would not have been good for them or for me. I would have tried to fix everyone's situations and tried to make sure everyone was doing well all of the time. At least that's what I did a lot when my kids were growing up. I would be exhausted and discouraged, because not everyone is going to be okay all of the time. Life is tricky, especially these days, and I've learned that it's okay to not always be okay. I've learned that there is beauty and maturity and growth in the pain. Who am I to take that away from anyone?

Having said that, it's hard when you're the mom and you've devoted your whole adult life to loving and coaching and nurturing your kids, and then they grow up and it's no longer your job. Can I get a witness?

Now, imagine living with them and seeing the reality of their lives, the ups and downs, up close and personal every day. It's an honor and privilege, and sometimes like today, it's a struggle.

In my work of helping myself and others overcome codependent behaviors, I've learned to ask three questions when struggling with worry or being overwhelmed by another person's problems or behavior. First, what is my problem or responsibility? Second, what is God's problem or responsibility? Lastly, what is their problem or responsibility?

These three questions have brought perspective and peace to my life. So often, in an effort to help someone, I take on a problem/situation that is not mine to carry. This not only disrespects the individual I am trying to help, but it is also frustrating because I do not have the ability to control another person's choices. So, taking a step back from the emotions of a situation and asking these questions helps me to know just what my role is in the situation. And most of the time, my role is to love and support the person and to pray for them.

So today, while I am feeling the weight of the reality of everyone's lives and all of the emotions that accompany them, I know that God sees us and He has each one of us in His mighty, loving hands. So, I take this moment, even now as I write, to invite Him into each situation. To ask Him to intervene on our behalves, to accomplish His will and purposes in each of our lives, and to tell Him how grateful I am to Him for this special time with my family.

Looking up

JULY 2020

August

2020
ENTRY ONE

Tonight's sunset was amazing. As I sit at my desk to write, the view of the moon, rising over the horizon and reflecting on the water, looks like a greeting card. Sometimes, living here feels a little bit like being in a Hallmark movie. Tonight is peaceful and gorgeous, and I am finally inspired to reflect upon the past few days and write about the other night, which was stressful and overflowing with adrenalin.

My oldest daughter, Carli, and her new husband, Cole, stopped in Colorado on their way to Michigan and picked up a little hitchhiker, a precious Goldendoodle puppy, Pepper. She is a delight, aside from a few stains on my new bedroom rug and the tumbleweeds of hair that I continually have to vacuum up (inevitable). She's learning to ring her bell to let us know she needs to go out. She stays in our yard and is learning to play fetch with her tennis ball. She is growing bigger by the day, and she's very sweet. We were all delighted to watch her when the newlyweds wanted to take an overnight trip to the west side of the state. What could happen, right?

The day was great, and we were all looking forward to a relaxing evening. It wasn't relaxing. After dinner, we headed outside to play cards. We were going to play euchre, a traditional Michigan card game, requiring only four people. There were five of us, so Jacob volunteered to fish while we played. That was when we heard it, "Pepper! No!" And she was off to the races, yipping and running, running and yelping. She had spotted the colorful fishing lure dangling from the pole Jacob was carrying and decided to eat it. She jumped up and grabbed it like she was a giant bass devouring her dinner. In a panic, she broke the line, but it was tangled with her paw so every time she ran it pulled in her mouth. This was very confusing for her and frustrating for us. We were all running around trying to stop her, and she was running to and then from each of us in fear and in pain. I can't imagine what we all sounded and looked like, running around screaming. Finally, Pepper stopped running and went to her favorite hiding place under the porch. There she was, just out of reach but looking at me with this pained, confused, scared look in her eyes. I lowered my voice. I slowly reached to gently touch her paw and told her it was going to be okay. She was going to be alright.

Gladly, she was okay. Eventually she trusted us enough and army crawled out to me. We clipped and unhooked what we could and took her to the vet for the rest. Three hours and $250 later, she was home and ready to sleep. The vet said she'd be just fine, and the next day, surprisingly, she was. Eating and drinking and playing like her old self. So when mommy and daddy got home, they had no idea the drama their sweet puppy had been through, and we were all happy to keep it that way.

No, I'm kidding. We told them everything, and they felt bad for Pepper and for us.

I've thought about all of us running around the yard trying to catch her. We wanted so badly to help her if she would have let us, but she was in a panic, and she didn't know what to do. If she would have come to one of us, we could have helped her so much sooner. I can't help but think about how we do that very same thing. We run around, stressing out about things we cannot fix on our own. We live in a state of fear and panic until we finally realize what we are doing isn't helping. It's actually doing us more harm than good. If we would just stop and crawl to Jesus, then He would hold us and untangle us. He is calling us by name, asking us to trust Him, knowing that in His hands we can always find comfort and healing.

ENTRY TWO

Yesterday, my family threw me a Hawaiian-themed graduation party. It was such a nice surprise to see all of the decorations. To hear the classic Hawaiian music and to receive my own colorful lai as I entered the room. It was even better to see my husband, all of my kids and their spouses, and my sweet momma waiting and smiling, just for me.

Everyone should have that feeling more than once in life. This celebration was a long time coming as several years ago, I started on a long and beautiful journey to receive my license as a Pastoral/Biblical Counselor. This program dug deep into the truth about what the Word of God says about who God is and what it says about who we are as His beloved children. It required a lot of reading and writing about what I had read, and it required presentations and prayer and many hours of training from a woman I greatly love and admire. It also included hours of class discussion with a group of women whose friendships I will cherish for life. When you learn how to finally get honest and vulnerable with a group of people, you tend to have a "fox hole" view of them. They saw and accepted my ugly moments, and I was present to see some of their's. We pushed through the cold winter months together, grieved the death of several friends together, and opened up about some painful and precious experiences that only the people in that room had the privilege of hearing. What a beautiful honor.

Ironically, the reason I started on this journey to become a counselor was because approximately five or six years ago, my adult daughters had both come home for a year after completing college and world traveling. They were both single, and dealing with the joys and disappointments from the above-mentioned experiences. After a time of empty nesting on my husband's and my part, let's just say this arrangement was a jolt back into family life. We all took turns displaying our frustrations and unhappiness until one Thanksgiving it all came to a head. It was during this holiday season I realized we needed help.

I'm so glad we went to counseling. We didn't go for long, but having the opportunity to share our perspectives and feelings with each other in a safe place with an objective, wise listener was money well spent. One of the most valuable things I've learned through the process of counseling and becoming a counselor is that there is beauty in the pain. Up until that point in my life, I'd avoided pain at all costs. I avoided it for myself, and I tried to shield my family from it whenever possible. I wanted everyone to be happy and positive all of the time, and if they weren't, I worked hard to fix the situation if possible. As you can imagine, this could be exhausting, and what I didn't realize was that by trying to make life pain-free, I robbed my family the opportunity of dealing with negative, difficult emotions. And I robbed God of being their source of healing and joy.

This goal of pain-free living kept us all from really feeling the sadness or grief or loneliness that life so often brings. As a believer in Christ, I also wanted to protect His image. As if He ever needed me to do that. But somewhere in my theology, I came to believe if you loved and dedicated your life to Jesus you would live a victorious life, full of blessing and peace. This belief system is true, but it is incomplete and definitely not honest. It works until someone you love dies after you've prayed or you get laid off or you don't get the part in the school play. Then what do you do? You soldier on with a smile on your face, confused, knowing that God is in control and that He loves you and has an amazing plan for your life but wondering where He was in the trial. At least that is where I was. I didn't appreciate the intimate, divine love that we experience in the trial, the maturity and growth it can usher in, and the peace and fellowship that occurs when we allow God to walk with us through the valley of the shadow of death, as stated in Psalm 23. I now appreciate and embrace the fact that we don't always get to avoid the valley and the shadows that come with living life in this broken world, and if we don't learn how to process our feelings and to express our thoughts and struggles honestly with our Lord and with others, we will hold them in or stuff them down until one day we are chronically depressed or grossly overweight or need just one more drink. It will come out somehow, someday.

I am grateful for the difficult year we had when we learned it was okay to not be okay. I'm grateful it taught me that denial isn't joy, and having the need to really trust God in the pain and in the tears gives Him the most amazing opportunity to meet us right there, smack dab in the middle of the yuck.

I can't begin to express how different the experience of living with my daughters is this time around. They are kind, thoughtful, honest, beautiful women who challenge me to be vulnerable, loving, and faith-filled, even during the difficult times of life.

ENTRY THREE

It was 1:32 a.m. on a Thursday morning when the smoke detector went off. I don't know why, but I immediately looked to see what time it was in an effort to understand how long we had been asleep. Needless to say, we all jumped out of bed in a panic, trying to assess the situation as adrenaline and unconsciousness mixed together like a bad cocktail. Because we are living in a newly renovated home, all of the smoke detectors are new and let me tell you, they are loud and freaky sounding. Along with the high-pitched alarm, we heard a synthetic voice repeat, "Fire! Fire! Fire!" Then, the bursts of sound continued.

I've never been in a fire, thank the Lord, but I have been subject to many fire drills, both in school as a student and then again many times as a substitute teacher. And while I've never experienced an actual fire, I have heard my kitchen smoke detector go off many, many times. Can we agree it doesn't take much to set one off? Burnt toast, liquid overflowing in the oven, the occasional burnt pan on the stove. I may have experienced this more than once as no one has ever compared me to Rachael Ray or Martha Stewart. The alarm sounded like it was from the starship Enterprise, and in the middle of the night with all of my people in the same house, I was fully awake pretty quickly.

We began searching for the smoke and ultimately the fire. Those of us on the second story could tell pretty quickly, as we peeked outside our bedroom doors, there was no fire or smoke upstairs. By the time I made it to the first floor, Mike and Cole had already made a sweep and had found nothing. That only left the basement apartment where my daughter, her husband, and sweet little baby boy live. It is a walkout basement with two windows, but there's something about them living on the lower level that makes me a little more trepidatious.

Thankfully, there was no smoke or fire down there either, and by the time we discovered this, we realized the alarm had stopped. Odd. Very odd.

The only other options were outside or the attic. We didn't see anything outside in the dark, and upon inspection, my husband realized that a detector was installed in the attic. Evidently as the battery wore down, we never heard the lovely chirping noise that warns you to change the battery. The cool and kind of freaky thing was, the detectors seemed to talk to each other. So, when the attic one finally died, the others took up the cause and warned us that there was a serious problem. You gotta love technology.

This event was exciting for all of us, with the exception of baby Silas. Thankfully, he slept right through it all. For me, it was extremely sobering. When something like this happens, you realize what could have happened. You realize that everyone you love most in the world is sleeping within these walls. It's wonderful and a little scary all at the same time. The good thing is this experience prompted us to put a plan in place, just in case there ever really is a fire.

Where are the fire extinguishers? How do they work? Where do we go once we are outside so we know if everyone made it out? All questions we did not have the answers to until this point.

By now, you know I like to make a spiritual connection between the events of my life and what the Word of God says, and this little story is full of potential. I could talk about one of my very favorite topics of prioritizing our relationship to Jesus as our source of power and strength. The passage of scripture found in John 15:1-11 illustrates the importance of abiding in the vine. I could talk about how the Lord will speak to us and give us merciful little warnings to help us come back to Him as our source, but we don't always pay attention or notice them. We continue to live exhausted, working to please God when everything we do should be an outpouring from our relationship of knowing Him, of living from Him as our source. I could go on all day about how we are not meant to live life alone and how we need people in our lives to help us see the dangers we often can't see on our own. I could go on and on about how our emotions are the indicator lights of our soul or how understanding that our emotions are a direct result of our thoughts and ultimately our belief system helps us navigate our way through negative emotions.

But I'm not going to do that (wink). What I am going to say is, "Thank you God that we are all healthy and here!"

I'm grateful

ENTRY FOUR

My girls and I spent the day together. We were having such a nice time eating lunch outside, shopping for little treasures and just enjoying the day together. It was a beautiful day that turned stormy. Literally and metaphorically speaking. The day did change quickly from hot and sunny to us grabbing our plates and running inside the restaurant to avoid the fat rain drops that began to fall. The weather changed as quickly as our moods.

Let me explain. After lunch, we headed to a large furniture store where we were wandering around, commenting, and dreaming about how fun it would be to purchase this couch for our living room or that gorgeous table for our dining room. Each piece was unique and beautiful, and it was fun to imagine being able to furnish our homes with the comfort and class this store could provide. As we were winding around the back of the store with no one within fifty feet of any of us, a sales woman approached me and asked me to pull my face mask up over my nose better. I don't want to add to the great mask debate of 2020, but the tone and obvious nit-picking of her demand, especially given we were the only people in the area, made my stomach start to turn. There is a way to make a request to someone and still maintain dignity and kindness. This was not it. As we drove home from the store, we attempted to navigate all of the feelings that accompanied the coronavirus wave that hit us once again. This season of lockdowns and quarantining, shutdowns and bad news has left us frustrated and exhausted. We have taken turns getting off social media and television, but at some point, we all encounter the voices from all sides, which are quickly making this year one for the record books.

"What is my role in all of this?" has been a question I've heard from family and friends more than once lately. I've been asking it myself as well. I am asking God how do I maintain peace and joy in the midst of what appears to be one of the craziest times in history, at least in my lifetime? Unfortunately, I do not have all of the answers as I sit at my computer with the need to start dinner pressing on my mind. But this is what I do picture. I picture Shadrach, Meshach and Abednego in the fiery furnace (see Daniel 3:16-28). The flames are surrounding them as they lift their hands in worship to the God whom they know and trust. Not only were they not consumed by the fire, but the smell of smoke was even repelled from their clothes. Man, that is how I want my life to look in the fiery furnace of 2020. I want to walk through the flames of confusion, sadness, loneliness, and fear without the smell of anger, bitterness, judgment, and negativity on me. Not pretending the fire isn't there, but maintaining my strength, peace and joy while surrounded by the flames. And I want to take people with me.

That's when I realized they were not alone. Jesus was with them in the fire, and whether they lived or whether they burned, they knew they would be okay because He was them. They were so confident in His goodness and faithfulness that they never bowed to the temptation of fear. They walked confidently into the fire, head held high, joy maintained. Today, as I sit on my bum, wet from the wave of frustration and anger that just plowed me over during my shopping experience, I look to the only one who can save me. The only one who will never leave me or reject me, Jesus. I rejoice that His Spirit lives in me and gives me the power and strength to face another day.

So, today I may not feel happy about what is happening in our world, but even as I write about what I know is true, I understand that if I keep walking, head held high, my hand in His, hopefully, I will enter 2021 not even smelling like smoke.

ENTRY
FIVE

"Be kind, for everyone is fighting their own battle," is a quote from Auggie the main character in the movie *Wonder*. Great movie with an amazing message. This quote jumped out at me when I watched it last night, as kindness has been on my mind a lot lately. Recently, Ellen DeGeneres and her producers have been under fire for making "Be kind" her slogan, while in reality, her employees spoke out sadly saying the opposite. It's one thing to encourage others to take the high road, be slow to criticize, and speak with words seasoned by grace, but it is another thing to actually do it ourselves. Why is it so easy to let the complaints and judgments fly, but so hard to give others the benefit of the doubt? If everyone would just think like we do, act like we do, and agree with us, life would be so much nicer. I say that jokingly, but isn't that honestly how we feel? I know it's how I feel much of the time, and it's virtually impossible to remain kind to others when this is my mindset.

As I ponder this truth and my desire to actually be kind not only to those whom I love and enjoy spending time with but also to those whom I don't know and who may directly oppose what I believe, my thoughts go to grace and humility. And I'm pondering which quality actually addresses this topic best. As I write, I realize grace and humility are twins. They are unique but are very much linked together. If we are actually going to live a lifestyle of kindness, we must walk in humility and cover those around us with grace.

But how do we do this? Especially in these tumultuous times. How do we live in such a way that others might be able to actually characterize us as kind? I'm pretty confident most of us desire to be characterized as kind by those who know us best. But if we honestly had the opportunity to ask those we encounter on a daily basis, would these people describe us that way? Our spouse? Our children? The person whose bumper we are riding, not because we are late but because they are not driving as fast as we would like them to? The cashier who is going to be at work all day and may have a conflict at home on her mind, so she is not rushing us through the line as fast as we would like? The friend on Facebook who is criticizing or arguing with an opinion we hold precious. I could go on and on. These examples were readily available for me to grab from my thoughts as they are all examples I wrestle with often.

I recently found two end tables for my newly renovated living room. I've been searching for just the right ones for weeks. Because the stores shut down due to Covid and then finally reopened, everyone was needing their shopping fix, myself included and the pickings were unusually slim. Going to the store during this time was another bizarre experience. Shelves, once filled with an abundance of selections, were now empty.

When I finally found what I was looking for, I joyfully and carefully transported my two new end tables home from the store. I took the corners unusually slow because every time I turned, the tables bumped into each other. To say I was driving like a very old lady would be fair. I can't help but wonder how many people behind me called me a name under their breaths as they were making glacial turns along with me and braking, way too soon before intersections.

I wonder if some were understanding and could imagine times when they themselves had to drive extra slow for a similar reason. I wonder if I would have. If I'm honest, it probably would depend on the day. Humility is an interesting thing. It's not weakness or insecurity, even though we sometimes think of it that way. In order for humility to have its complete work, it seems to me there must be a security and confidence in our identity. When we know we are valued and loved by God, it's easier for us to see others that way as well. And when I say we know we are valued and loved by God, I'm talking about having a revelation—that time or times when we have experienced His love and we better understand our value because it has been revealed to us by the Spirit of God. When we are living from that place of love and acceptance, it's so much easier to honor others and treat them with grace and kindness. Oddly, it begins with us, our thoughts about ourselves, then it flows out to others.

It's a rough world out there, and it feels like it's getting rougher. All of us are dealing with something — debt, job security, a child who is struggling and health concerns just to name a few. All of which can lead to the long term effects of depression and anxiety. I don't know about you, but I'm with Auggie. I want to remember to be kind to those I come in contact with today. Who knows what battle they may be facing?

ENTRY SIX

I just got back from a week-long vacation in Tahoe. Mike and I went with some amazing, lifelong friends. It is the first time we have gotten away in a long time, and while we were not alone, there is something special about pressing the pause button and getting away from the cares of the world together, especially given our current circumstances.

Traveling during a pandemic, or whatever you might call what this is turning in to, is interesting to say the least. Airports and planes are half-empty. We had to wear a mask for the full flight from Michigan to California. Everyone is encouraged to stay away from each other. It's all so odd. Walking through the airport today, I heard a recording over the loud speaker. It was a monotone female voice telling me to stay away from others and keep my mask on at all times, among other restrictive instructions. I felt like I was in a futuristic zombie movie about the end of the world. I don't mean to sound dramatic, but with all of the science fiction movies I've seen, this is as close as I've ever come to starring in one.

I'm noticing people don't look me in the eye as much as they used to, and they sure don't talk to me as much. I'm not a super social person, but I am quick to give a compliment if I see a women with a cute hair style, amazing purse, or adorable child. I do speak to strangers in a friendly, casual way, but this social distancing thing is really starting to take its toll on me. I've noticed I have to be overly friendly when I speak to anyone if I want to get a response, and I can't help but wonder what the long-term ramifications are going to be if all of us aren't able to be social again soon. I get it though. People are afraid. If you spend an abundance of time watching the news or on social media, you see things you never thought would happen, and it is scary.

Thinking back over this week, I'm so grateful for our amazing friends. Even with all of the restrictions, we swam and laughed and played cards and ate and hiked and then ate some more. We shopped and prayed and sang and marveled at God's great handiwork together. You get the picture. We continued to "do life" together. I think maybe this vacation was even sweeter because for the past five months, we went weeks at a time without seeing each other in person. We all hunkered down and did what we needed to do in order to stay healthy. We reached out to our families and neighbors, making sure that no one went without food or necessities, and we stayed home and to ourselves for the most part. So, having the unusual opportunity to spend a week together was good medicine. For sure.

If you've read my book, *Death of a Church Lady, Confessions of Hurt, Healing & Freedom* or any of my blogs (shameless plug), you know that I can only go so long before I bring up the topic of community. It's essential to our well-being, and frankly, it's hard to go and reach anybody with the Gospel if you don't have relationships with them. Jesus told us we are to love God and love our neighbor as ourselves. Kind of hard to do if you have never met your neighbor or are not willing to talk to that person whom you could potentially be neighborly to. I don't mean to preach. I'm just very passionate about relationships. At age fifty-five, I now understand more than ever that being a Christian is not about following a set of rules or doing good things to please God. It's about relationship. It's about love and being made new. It's about receiving love and forgiveness from Him first and then letting it complete who you are so it can spill onto others.

I cherish the time I had with my precious friends this week. I will remember this trip forever. I also treasure the new friends I am making and the literal neighbors I have yet to meet, and I am grateful for all of the time I am able to spend with my amazing children during this unique season. Basically, I'm grateful for all of the relationships I have. I wouldn't be who I am without them. They bring wisdom and correction, love and laughter into my life. They are the hands and feet and often the voice of Jesus to me. And hopefully I am to them as well.

It's good to be home

AUGUST 2020

September

2020
ENTRY ONE

We're having a party tomorrow. We are finally getting to celebrate Carli and Cole's wedding. We've been planning for and anticipating it since they got married back in March in California. My how things can change in a year. Last year at this time, they were both living in California, dating, and working different jobs. Today, they are living with us here in Michigan, married with a baby on the way. The year 2020 didn't slow them down.

The preparations have been quite exhausting as the house we purchased has been in disrepair for almost twenty years. Picture *The Adams Family* meets *Fixer Upper*. That's what our house looked like when we started. Trees and shrubs were overtaking the property. Mold and grime covered the house and we needed to replace the entire roof. Looking at it today, it's obvious we've all put many, many hours and dollars into making it look clean and updated. And while it's been a lot of work, today we are reaping the benefit.

The tent and dance floor got put up today in front of the water. It's just sitting there, waiting for the love, joy, and laughter that will soon fill it. While I can picture the beauty and fun that will take place tomorrow, today I'm exhausted. Afternoon is turning into evening, and we are all quickly running out of steam. Pizza and a cold drink are enabling us to go into the evening hours. Everyone is working to make the celebration as beautiful as possible, and honestly, we are all trying to help Mike get through his list of things that must be done outside before we entertain.

His list is not necessarily everyone else's list, as he has a real eye for landscaping, but the rally continues as we can see light at the end of the wood-chopping, flower-potting, light-fixing, table-setting tunnel. We've done the work, and soon, we get to enjoy the fruit of our labor.

In a world of Facebook, Instagram, and Kardashians, we're used to seeing the final product, and oftentimes, we see it with a filter and a little Photoshop, removing the imperfections. We look at what others are doing and wonder why our lives don't look like that. What we usually don't take into account are the hours spent in the gym, hours spent in prayer, or the backache that is a result of hours of pulling weeds. It doesn't matter what it is, all good things take effort. It's just life.

I love what Joyce Meyer says, "Success doesn't feel like success". That's because success takes a lot of work, and when it is on display, only the person or group of people experiencing it know what it took to actually get there.

Tomorrow when our guests arrive, most of them will never know the teamwork and long hours it took to get our property looking like it does for the party, and that's okay with us. We'll know, and we will enjoy the beauty of it all that much more because we know what it took to get it ready with sweat and unity and a common goal. And when we see Carli and Cole receiving their guests with smiles on their faces, we'll know it was worth it all.

So today, I go to bed tired and sore and excited for tomorrow.

ENTRY TWO

You've seen *Father of the Bride*, right? Well, this evening was as close as I'll ever get to being in that movie. The weather was perfect. The flowers were stunning. The dance floor and backyard were covered in lights. The food was amazing, especially because I didn't have to make it. Music filled the air, and so many of the people we love were standing in our front yard or backyard. I can't get used to lake living lingo. After all the planning, it was time to enjoy the moment and celebrate love.

Covid-19, Rona, the pandemic, whatever term you use, has taken a toll on all of us. If isolation and fear weren't enough, add civil unrest and a political tsunami, not to mention unemployment and fires and whatever else may have impacted your little corner of the world. This year has been crazy, and it's not over yet. I bring all of that up to say, I think this time together was even more special because we've been starving for human contact for so long.

Scripture tells us in 2 Timothy 1:7, "God has not given us a spirit of fear and timidity, but of power, love and self-discipline". Living in this atmosphere of fear and isolation is counter-intuitive to how we were made to live, so I think this event had a special dose of joy and appreciation because we were finally together again. We were missing many people who didn't feel comfortable traveling or being out in a group. Our hearts ached for them to be with us. For many of us, it was the first time in a long time we put our fancy clothes on, got dolled up, and took some time to not worry about the future or talk politics. We were just there, in the moment, celebrating two young people who desired to honor God so much they sacrificed their conventional wedding to be together. What a beautiful reason.

Having the opportunity to witness my new son sit back and look at my expecting daughter with such affection, peace, and joy during the reception, confirmed what I already knew. God brought them together. This moment of contemplation was like another brick that was laid in the foundation of my faith and trust in God. He continually reminds me that He's got me and all of us covered.

As we watched the orange harvest moon rise over the water, we all stopped for a moment and marveled at the beauty of God's creation. And as we ended the evening with fireworks over the water, I was filled with joy and contentment, knowing we had done all that we could to make our daughter and our new son-in-law feel loved and special. That was the goal. To let two people know that we see them, love them, and honor them. To communicate that we are with them and behind them, come what may.

Who knows what the future holds? I write with trepidation, knowing that these are unusually tumultuous times and the events that fill the rest of this book could be scary or sad. I just don't know. So for now, I will pause to enjoy the memory of a great day with the people I love on the lake.

ENTRY THREE

Yesterday was tough. It was a beautiful, sunny Sunday, and I had every reason to be happy. But I had to push through sadness all day long. Life continues to be way different than it was before, and I'm struggling to navigate through it with joy, peace, and strength. At least today. Most of the time, I'm fine. I live my life as normally as possible. I try to limit the amount of time I spend watching the news and on social media, and I take every opportunity to do normal, everyday things. Living with this precious group certainly helps keep me busy and engaged, that's for sure.

But today, I'm feeling blue because church just isn't the same, and I'm really, really missing the corporate worship and fellowship that accompanies attending church, in person, like the good old days. My church has opened back up. We started meeting in our cars on the grass a few months ago, and we have recently graduated to "back in the building" worship; however, you have to register, and there are so many restrictions it kind of makes me sad when I am there. Don't move around. No hugging or talking inside. Exit in different directions. I know it's meant to keep us all healthy, but it's still hard for my heart to adjust.

All of the services at our church were full yesterday, so I couldn't register for a spot. We either had to stay home (again) and watch online or try a different church. I thought it would be fun to try a new one closer to home. It wasn't. It made me sad. The church we visited will remain anonymous, but it is named for the light and glory of the Lord. Unfortunately, the auditorium was hollow and dark inside. It made me sad. As I walked into the mostly empty church and looked into the dark, foggy auditorium where people sat separated from one another with masks on (required), I couldn't do it. I couldn't go sit in the dark, isolated, even while surrounded by people; so we turned back around and headed into the sunlight.

I felt guilty for feeling this way, as people in some countries walk for miles to worship, but I knew God didn't want me to feel guilt or shame. He wanted to change my heart or at least minister to my heart. He's good like that. So, Mike and I went for coffee and stopped at Home Goods for a little shopping therapy. (Don't judge me.) For the rest of the day, I've had to continually ask the Lord to renew my mind and help me to think differently about this season we are currently in. I understand that 2020 is a crazy year and feeling all of the feels that accompany this kind of unprecedented trial is a natural and even healthy thing to do. At the end of the day though, I realized there are things out of my control. I can either pray for change and peace, or I can be frustrated that the world around me is not operating as I would like it to.

This is an ongoing process. I know. And resting and allowing the Holy Spirit to bring truth and perspective to my heart and mind is what I need to do continually.

In the afternoon, I reached out to some friends who came over in the evening and we spent time talking around the fire. We shared about our personal challenges to stay positive in such a tumultuous environment. It felt good to know I'm not alone in the struggle. It was helpful to have others remind me that God has everything under control and this too shall pass. We prayed for each other and our kids while sitting around the fire. It filled my heart, like community and prayer always does.

Today, I'm feeling lighter. It's still a struggle, this battle in my mind, but I'm not giving in to it. I'm pressing on. I'm seeking first the Kingdom and asking God for more of His Spirit in my life. I'm reading my Bible. I'm doing what I can to walk this thing out, keeping my testimony and sharing the love of Jesus as I do. I'm looking forward to getting together again with our dear friends to pray and praise. It's good medicine.

ENTRY FOUR

What a day! My adorable, sweet grandson turned one today. My how the time has flown. I feel like this year is on fast forward. I guess because I've been busy, first with fixing up the house, then everyone moving into the house, then working on the outside of the house. By the time I help with the baby or go grocery shopping again, it's time for dinner. It's all great stuff, but it's all happening so fast.

Writing this little memoir helps me to stop and take it all in. I'm glad for that. As I sit at my desk and look out the window, the sky is reflecting pink on the water, and my husband is on the water's edge trying to catch that giant fish that keeps jumping out of the water in front of our house, just to taunt us. I'm pretty sure none of us will catch him this year, but it sure is fun and relaxing to try.

It's funny what a big deal the first birthday is. I remember having family and friends over for my kids' first birthday parties. Looking at little Silas today, I realize that he's not a baby anymore. He's pulling himself up and contemplating taking a step or two, but not yet. He's so aware of what's happening around him and beginning to communicate. It's precious to watch, and up until today, I hadn't noticed how old he looks. Young enough to cling to his bottle and old enough to reach for my French fries. As I pause to think about the day, the friends who joined us, the extended family who all showed up to love us and show support, I am grateful,

grateful that today we are all here and healthy.

The Blessing by Kari Jobe, Cody Carnes and Elevation Worship was playing today as we were getting ready for the party, and Silas got a kick out of me singing it to him and waving my hands over him declaring, "And your children, and their children, and their children... May His presence go before you and behind you and beside you." He really giggled when I swirled my hands around his body at the "all around you" part. He thought I was just singing and playing with him, but as I waved my hands towards him, in the Spirit, I was declaring blessings and health and favor over his life. I'm so grateful that I get to be here to watch him grow and show him the love of God. I don't take it for granted.

I remember my momma rocking me in the white leather rocking chair by our front door when I was a little towheaded child. She would make up these "little ditties," incorporating my name, like her daddy did for her. "T-E-R-I spells sweetness. T-E-R-I spells love. T-E-R-I spells Teri. Gift from the Lord above." One generation impacting another. I look at my children and the love and truth that they possess. They are learning or have learned things that I didn't get until I was in my late forties. They are the recipients of the fruit produced from generations of Christ followers. I know that can sound prideful, but I realize now more than ever the ripple effect our lives have had on those around us. Mike and I have received God's grace and forgiveness and love. We have stepped out of the shadows of shame and regret and are now walking in truth, and as vulnerability works, it encourages those around us to do the same.

We are far from perfect, that is for sure. We are a work in progress, I will readily admit, but here we are, surrounded by three generations, huddled in this big 'ole house. Here for the tears and here for the laughter and everything in between. It's dark now as I look outside my window. I can see my kids by the fire. I think I will join them.

ENTRY FIVE

We could have died. Last night, my daughter and I were heading back from a meeting with her midwife when within seconds our lives were at risk, and then it was over. One moment. That is how quickly everything could have changed.

At her appointment, we got to hear baby girl's heartbeat, and it took me by surprise how emotional I got when I heard it for the first time. Carli has begun her third trimester, and her baby bump is growing as perfectly as it should. I've even felt the baby kick, so I'm not sure why when I heard that magical swishing sound, tears immediately filled my eyes. I could hear the life inside my daughter. What a precious gift. The midwife is almost two hours away, but the conversation, Starbucks, and podcasts made the time fly by.

We were having a great conversation on the way home when it happened. Out of nowhere, literally nowhere, a car came flying past me and cut in front of me so close that he clipped my front left bumper. It all happened so fast I didn't even notice him until his bumper had clipped mine, making the car rock for a minute. I held the wheel steady, and before I knew it, he was passing in front of me, almost driving perpendicular to the freeway. My cruise was set on 78. I was looking straight ahead. And both of my hands just happened to be at ten and two. As he clipped me, instinct kicked in, and I just held the car in place as we processed what had just happened. When we watched him speed to the exit, the first words out of my mouth were, "Thank you, Lord."

It could have been so different. There are

many other choice words I could have said in that moment. God surely knows (wink), but somehow, I understood the severity of the situation immediately. If he had been going one mile an hour slower, if I hadn't been paying attention, the shock of him hitting me could have caused me to overcompensate or swerve drastically. He could have rolled. I could have rolled. The several cars that were behind me could have pushed us to the other side of the road. There are a thousand different things that could have happened, but all that did happen was a little bit of paint being scraped off my car, and he made it across all FOUR lanes.

One moment could have changed so many lives. It happens every day. Experiences like this one make me pause and slow down to treasure how beautiful and fragile our lives really are. It reminds me what is really important, and for me, that's always a good thing. Days like this reveal how little control we actually have. They make me appreciate today because we just never know what tomorrow holds.

Ten and two baby

October

2020
ENTRY ONE

    I have some friends who are making a huge impact for the Kingdom. My friends Joy and Tara at Barn 45 (Barn45.org) are on Facebook Live every morning Monday through Friday, reading and discussing the Word of God. It has been amazing to watch what started at the beginning of the Covid-19 lockdown as two friends connecting in their sweatshirts from home grow to thousands of people watching them live on Facebook and/or later on YouTube.

    This morning, they were talking about the seasons of life and how we have the tendency to avoid pain by sticking our heads in the sand or steering clear of difficult times at all costs. I thought to myself as

I listened, we desire our lives to look like San Diego where it's 70 degrees and sunny all of the time. But life is more like living in Michigan with its four seasons, some comfortable and sunny and others drenched by freezing rain, gray skies, and snow-covered roads. We have the choice to pull the covers over our heads and avoid the dark days of winter, or we can put our boots on and go for a walk to catch the fall colors or to walk through a beautiful snow-covered meadow. But if we are expecting Michigan to look like California, we will live in a constant state of disappointment.

As Joy and Tara were speaking, I was dusting my office/bedroom as the sun was streaming through the window, highlighting all of the dust and tumbleweeds or whatever it is that so quickly manifests under my desk and dressers. As I listened, I couldn't help but notice the parallel between what I was doing in the physical and what they were talking about in the spirit. When my room is dark, it feels like my room is clean, and I am content to sit on my bed and read or watch TV. I'm comfortable not dealing with the dust in the dark because I don't deal with what I can't see; however, when the sun brings its intense light into my room, it exposes all of the layers of dirt and grime that were there all along, much like the Holy Spirit does in my heart, and I'm left with a choice. Now that I see what's really there, will I take the time to deal with it or will I ignore it? Will I allow the light of God's Word to speak correction and/or encouragement to my heart?

Will I repent and receive His never-ending, powerful forgiveness? Or, will I shut the door and walk away? I've done both, but I've learned to love those times when God lovingly works in my heart. I've learned to yield to Him because I know I can trust Him – always. So, when the sun is shining in and the light makes it easy to see where the dirt is, which can be uncomfortable because I can't believe I let it get so dusty, I push through the shame and embarrassment, knowing when I am done and everything is fresh and clean, it will look and feel really good.

As I continued to watch, there was a woman on the chat who made a comment about how she avoids the difficulties of life and numbs out by using alcohol to help her cope. She shuts the door so to speak. I admired her confession, and I could relate to her so well. I don't use alcohol, but I have used food, and going to the movies, and watching TV to avoid feeling difficult emotions. If I'm honest, I've lived most of my life never wanting to feel sad or lonely or angry. Like many of us, I was never taught what to do with those emotions. I tried to look on the bright side. I tried to think of my cup as being half full. I did what Philippians 4:8 told me to do, "Fix your thoughts on what is true, and honorable, and right, and pure, and lovely, and admirable. Think about things that are excellent and worthy of praise." While this has served me well and is a great way to live, it is not a license to avoid reality or truth.

I've learned that getting honest with myself and others can sometimes lead to sadness, loneliness, or anger. It can be painful for a while, but the fruit of feeling the pain and inviting God and possibly a trusted loved one into my world has brought a healing and freedom I didn't know existed. Dr. Phil says, "You can't change what you don't acknowledge." I can see how the conversation between Tara and Joy regarding 2 Timothy 4 was used as a light for this woman to illuminate something that she didn't want to see. She realized that drinking was keeping her from feeling and the lack of feelings was keeping her from facing issues that were right in front of her. I can imagine this avoidance only prolonged the inevitable and, many times, compounded her issues. Finally getting honest with herself and then with others during the live chat was very brave. Not only did it encourage others to be vulnerable, but I believe it let the light into her struggle and was the first step toward her freedom and healing. Now that the light of God's Word was illuminated in this area of her life, she could allow the Holy Spirit to help her deal with the feelings and the situations that had caused her so much pain. James 5:16 says it this way, "Confess your sins to each other and pray for each other so that you may be healed."

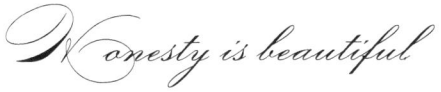

Honesty is beautiful

ENTRY TWO

We bought a day bed for our fourth bedroom/nursery/guest room upstairs. We've had a guest sleep in it almost every night since its arrival. Carli's friends from California surprised her and came to Michigan for her baby shower. Then, a few weeks ago, my nephew Tyler stayed with us for a few nights. It's so nice to have the extra space because some of our most precious times happen at night around the fire outside or while we pile in the living room late in the evening for a movie. Having this extra space makes it possible for a guest to stay, and with eight people living here already, that's pretty cool.

My momma recently came and stayed for several nights before her eighty-fifth birthday party. She's been looking forward to staying longer than an afternoon, so it was the perfect time to host her. And, yes, we had another party. Having such a big yard and outside space has really helped with the possibility of having people over. Thankfully, for the most part, all of our events have had great weather, which has given everyone room to move around. The birthday party for my mom was the first time the whole family has been together since Covid hit. It was her birthday wish for all of us to be together, and this time, no one was missing. We were all there, from my eighty-five-year-old mom to our little thirteen-month-old Silas. What a joy it was to watch all of the little cousins run around the yard, playing with balloons and with each other. Laughing, crying (when a balloon got away and disappeared into the clouds), and getting to know one another again. It was precious. It was family. It was a long time coming.

It hasn't been just this pandemic that's kept us apart. It's been nearly impossible to get everyone together. On my mom's eightieth birthday, we all went to Mackinac Island together, but we were missing three of us. It was impossible for those who lived out of state to make it, so this time together was extra special. My mom had every one of her children, their spouses, and all of their kids together in one place, at one time, just for her.

She told me she wanted to say something before Mike prayed for our meal. She mentioned it to me several times, so I knew it was heavy on her mind. When the time came for us to eat, we gathered in the kitchen, and she told us all again what Jesus has meant to her life. She told us that the one thing she wanted when she got to heaven was to be able to greet each of us when it is our time to leave this earth. She took me by surprise when she had us take a moment of silence to contemplate our lives and, if we hadn't already, to give our lives fully to Jesus. As you can imagine, the Spirit of God fell in that room, and I was moved not only by His presence but by her faithfulness to make sure not one of us missed out on the best decision we could ever make.

After eating and taking a family picture by the lake, we made our way to the living room. Before arriving, I asked everyone to write a little something to tell Mom/Grandma/Great Grandma Barb what she means to each of us. It could be a poem, a memory, a letter, whatever. Then because she is losing her eyesight to Macular Degeneration, we recorded this time of us sharing our letters with her. Why do we wait until someone is gone to really tell them what they mean to us? We didn't want the opportunity of us all being together to go by without letting her know the impact she has made on all of our lives.

As you can imagine, we laughed and we cried. We took our time reading poems and recalling stories of years gone by. It was amazing, and we have it recorded for her to listen to when she is all alone in her condo remembering. My brother sang and cried, my nieces' and nephews' children tried to say something meaningful as they mustered up their young courage. Everyone's words were precious. It was very healing and encouraging for all of us to hear from one another. Some memories and statements were funny, and some were tender and sentimental. It was obvious to all of us that we are blessed. We are all blessed because one woman and one man stayed married for over fifty years. They made it through times of abundance and also great need. It wasn't a perfect marriage, because no one is perfect, but they surely were committed to the Lord, to each other, and to their children. They loved fiercely, and while my sweet daddy has gone to be with the Lord, my mother continues to carry on with grace and optimism.

I was touched by hearing my children share their hearts and declare their love to my mom. They have grown to become such amazing people, and it had to take courage for my new sons-in-law to get in front of their new family and share, but they did it with sincerity and charm. I'm one blessed momma.

My nephew Tyler said something in his letter when sharing his great love and appreciation for his mamaw. It was a full-circle moment from the statement she made before we ate. He said when he makes it to the end of his life and he makes it to the pearly gates, he's going to say, "I'm with Barb." That statement brought the room to life with laughter and recognition. His statement wasn't theological. Of course, the only reason we make it to heaven is because of Jesus. Period. But because of the impact she has made for the kingdom through the way she has lived her life and the impact she has as she enters a room, his statement was perfect, and we could all relate.

That was the last party for a while. I hope. But my

heart is full as I recall all of the blessed events we've had the opportunity to host on this new property this summer and fall. It is not the last company we will host though. My mother-in-law came to town yesterday. She is staying with us for the week. I better get downstairs.

Time for dinner

ENTRY THREE

I just got off the phone with one of my longest and best friends. She just informed me that she has a mass on her ovary and will most likely be getting a hysterectomy soon. The reality of her words is rolling around in my head like a giant marble in my brain as I sit down to write. As we spoke, she shared the most optimistic prognosis, and we both agreed this is what we are hoping and praying for. Then she voiced her greatest fear. The thing neither one of us wanted to say out loud. The big C. The daunting unknown future. The surreal moment when you realize your life is possibly going to change forever. As we spoke, the distance between us grew as I wanted to reach out and hug her. To sit across the table with her, a cup of coffee or Diet Coke in hand like we've done a thousand times before. To process and just to be together. But all I could do was listen and talk some more, and try to make her laugh because it beats the alternative of crying. We ended up doing both, as I've learned the value of each. Just to feel it. Sit with it. Grieve it. It was the only medicine I could offer her today.

She was recently in Michigan visiting, and one of the birthday parties we had hosted was to celebrate her fiftieth. She and her family moved south about six years ago, but even with all of the miles between us, we have continued to stay connected and have seen each other every few months. It's not the same, having her several states away. I miss the ease that proximity allows.

I miss the relationship that common interests breed; the people you see every day because you go to the same place or do the same thing. The faces you see at church on Sunday and then again for a meal, or small group, or choir practice. We take having the opportunity to do life together for granted, until it's taken away. With this crazy pandemic, even the most normal interactions have been limited. I know after this year, I will forever treasure the people I love and enjoy being with more than I ever have.

I've been blessed to have an amazing group of

friends to worship and serve with, vacation with, and raise my children alongside. I realize the treasure these friends and my family are. It's unusual for people to stay in the same place long enough to grow deep relational roots. It's the reason I didn't want to move unless the Lord directly told me to. These friends, my sister, and the rest of my family are like precious gold in my life.

When this precious friend moved, I lived in denial for years. It took me years to make peace with the fact that she and her family had moved on to the journey God had called them to, but I have this hope, deep in the quiet place of my soul that we will someday live near to each other once again, enabling us many more opportunities to linger over that cup of coffee while discussing the tender dreams and struggles of our hearts.

This brings me back to today's conversation with her. My heart aches as I contemplate our unknown futures—as I ponder all of the hopes and dreams we share, wanting to minister to marriages and families together. The time we hope to spend enjoying lunches and shopping with grandkids and all of the usual things we enjoy doing together. We have too much to experience together. So, today I will pray; and tomorrow, I will pray again for her health and life. I will be present with her to journey on this next road, right by her side, like she has done for me so many times before. I will trust that God is good and He has got her. I will rely upon His Word, and I will call upon His name.

As we were ending our conversation over FaceTime this morning, the James Taylor song "You've Got a Friend" popped into my head, and with tears welling up in both of our eyes, I felt compelled to sing, "You just call out my name, and you know wherever I am. I'll come running, to see you again..."

ENTRY FOUR

The sky is gray today. The air is cold, and as I sit at my desk to write, I feel like a little old grandma with a blanket on my lap. When you live in Michigan, you do whatever you can to stay toasty and warm. It is, however, the best-smelling time of year, in my opinion. Candles are burning, filling the rooms with pumpkin spice and cinnamon. Those yummy smells mix with the sweet smell of coffee or hot chocolate or perhaps a roast in the oven.

All of these smells take me back to my youth and the days when I was a young momma and had my first home. What a thrill it was to furnish it all on my own. Creating atmosphere is something I've always been passionate about. Having music on, yummy food, and candles are common in my home. I know I'm not the only one who enjoys and pays attention to atmosphere. Who doesn't like to be surrounded by the sights and smells of the good times?

Coincidentally, my hubby just brought me a cup of homemade hot chocolate. "I thought you might enjoy something sweet," he said as he set it down on my desk in front of me and walked away with a smile. Yummy, and timely.

The topic of fall makes me think of watching Michigan football. Now that is a prominent memory from my childhood. My father was a diehard Wolverine fanatic. He used to wake us up on Saturday mornings by playing the Michigan fight song full blast on his record player. Yes, a record player. And yes, I am that old. The fact that he had the marching band's album reveals what a Michigan junkie he really was. As I write, I realize that my love for music and setting an atmosphere just might have been inherited from my daddio. My mom and dad were season ticket holders along with a substantial group of their friends. I can recall many beautiful fall afternoons when a friend and I would tag along and enjoy the treats found on a tailgate, watch the band march in with the sound filling the giant stadium, and spend more time playing out in the area surrounding the stadium than actually watching the game. Tickets were only ten bucks back then, so it was no biggie that exploring was more interesting to us than watching two hours of football.

I've always been nostalgic about fall, and I'm pretty sure football has a lot to do with that. The virus almost kept football from happening this year. In my fifty-five years, I'm pretty sure that's never been contemplated before. Thankfully, they are playing, albeit much later this year, but I don't care. I'm just happy it's happening.

My sweet daddy passed away seven years ago, and during the first year after his death, I didn't truly cry until I attended the first game that season. I walked into the stadium and heard that band start to play, and whoosh, that was it. Just the thought of it fills my eyes with tears again.

That's what memories do. They take us back. They can trigger great joy, or they can cause us to pause, causing us to grieve a little bit more. Some waves of grief are large and can sweep our feet out from under us. While others are small ripples, yet they sting with surprising intensity. My daddy wasn't a perfect man. No man is. I have had to deal with some of the lies I've believed about myself as a result of my relationship with him. I've learned recently the value of looking back at my life honestly. For many years, I "covered" the unhealthy areas of his life and how they affected me, thinking it was the Christian thing to do, but I've learned the havoc that denial or minimizing something can cause the soul (mind, will, and emotions). How can I forgive something I deny ever happened? Why do I need to forgive if it wasn't that bad? I can't, but that doesn't mean it doesn't affect my life. It is not until I get honest and stop pretending that I can look at the reality of what the situation was, and acknowledge that it caused me pain. Only when I say that my parent or grandparent or whomever it was that hurt me, lived a flawed and often sinful life can I take an honest look at my past and finally let go of needing to get justice for myself or a loved one and truly forgive. I know it seems obvious, but I feel compelled to say, we cannot forgive or let go of what we don't acknowledge. Anger, resentment, and bitterness can simmer on low beneath the surface of our lives, and we don't even realize they're there, let alone understand how it got there, until we are willing to get honest. God has something better for us. He wants to free us from the toxic ties that hold us, sometimes unconsciously, to our past hurts.

Well, that got deep quickly. I didn't expect to go there when I started writing today. I am trusting the Spirit of God as I write. He knows the hands that will hold this book. Who knows, maybe it's just for me. If so, it remains to be *Time Well Spent*. Thank you Lord for always leading me to places I would not or could not get to on my own.

ENTRY FIVE

I voted in the presidential election today. Election day isn't until next week, but a lot of people are voting absentee and turning it in immediately, so I thought I would do the same to avoid the lines on Tuesday. There had to have been at least ten other people voting along with me in the short time I was there.

I'll admit, I was nervous leaving my vote in the box by the door. How crazy to think that something could happen and my vote wouldn't count. I am a little anxious about it, but I've got to trust the system at some point. It seems like many of the experiences of living in 2020 are life imitating art. I've seen too many television shows where an election is stolen and the "bad guys" win. I am hoping and praying this election day will be peaceful, and the transfer of power, if there is one, will be just and smooth.

This election is unique to say the least. I didn't even know you could vote early, with the exception of absentee, until this year. Who would want to do that anyway? I've always just woken up on the designated Tuesday in November and waited in a moderately long line to cast my vote, just like everyone else. This year is so much more intense. Both sides agree this decision will have extreme ramifications for our country's future, and as with any conflict, both sides feel justified and passionate about their argument. I know I am passionate about mine.

I am grateful for the freedom this country provides. I do see some of our liberties at risk, and to say it concerns me is putting it way too mildly. It has prompted me to vote three days early. I realize I haven't given much thought to what believers in China, North Korea, Iran, and other communist/socialist countries have had to endure, often facing lifelong jail times or even death for their faith in Christ. They don't get to vote – about anything. With certain liberties at risk, I am prompted to pray for them now more than ever.

OCTOBER 2020

November

2020
ENTRY ONE

I got tested for Covid yesterday. It came back negative, but I'm having my doubts. I've been hanging out in my room for two days now, and honestly, I think I've needed the rest. I've got a cough and a very low fever, but I'm rarely sick. I'm feeling a little bit like a baby; however, with a pregnant daughter and an elderly momma, I feel like I can't be too careful. I'm going to take this time to watch some chick flicks and rest. I'd like to use this time to get some of my reading done. I've got several books on the corner of my desk that I keep intending to read. I'm just not sure I've got the energy to focus right now.

I wrote the previous paragraph almost a week ago.

My fever has persisted and I've been in a fog for days. My days have been filled with chills, so I take a bath. Then I start a movie and eventually end up dozing off. I wake up with what I would describe as hot skin that eventually transitions to chills, so I take another bath. On the bright side, I have had the chance to catch up on many of my old DVDs and my rest. I finally feel good enough to sit at my desk and write, thanks to a healthy dose of Motrin. I'm normally a very healthy person, thank God. I don't get sick very often, and when I do, I'd like to think I'm pretty tough. I've had to be tough. Ask any mom. Having children doesn't allow for time off to recover. The kids wake up and need—and they keep needing until it's time for bed.

I've had the occasional cough or cold, but I must confess, this fever is kicking my butt. I've only had a mild temperature, but it makes my head pound, my skin hurt, and my muscles ache. I don't know, it seems like all of these symptoms are Covid. I am going to get another test tomorrow. I would have gone again sooner, but it's been difficult to get an appointment.

As I'm writing today, I'm only writing a little bit at a time. I'm having a difficult time focusing, so I'm taking a break every few paragraphs. Fun new fact, I've lost my ability to smell. It's the oddest thing. I didn't know I couldn't smell until my daughter said, "Did you smell that?" Earlier today. I couldn't smell what she was referring to, so I've been experimenting. I've cleaned with Clorox. Nothing. I lit my favorite candle. Nothing. I used my favorite soap. Nope. I've heard a common symptom of the coronavirus is losing your sense of taste and smell, but I've also heard that is more common with the younger crowd. Maybe I should be happy I'm hanging with the youngins on this one. I'm also wondering if I should get a quarter pounder and fries for dinner if my taste is the next to go. At least I still have my sense of humor. See what I did there?

Me being sick is so much bigger than me just being sick. With all of us living together in one house, it affects so many lives. Carli's pregnant. I sure don't want her to get it. The guys are all working outside of the house. I sure don't want them to get it. I don't want Mallory and Silas to get it either, but from the very beginning, it was obvious that with how contagious this virus is we all will encounter it at some point. It's just very weird keeping to myself up here in my room. As I am contemplating my next thought, I see my daughter go into the yard to wash out her kitchen garbage can with the hose. I stop what I'm doing, and I pray for her. For God to bless her and give her joy during this difficult season. Now my son is down by the lake, building a fire in the pit while the dog is chewing on yet another piece of wood next to him. I stop to pray for him as well. I ask God to reveal Himself to him in a greater way. I pray he would know the Father's love in a tangible way, more than he ever has before. I also ask that he would be in health and walk in truth.

As I'm finishing this entry, my head is getting a little dizzy, so I'm going back to bed. Before I do, I whisper another prayer. "Father, thank you that You are with me. Thank you that You see me up here in my room all on my own but never alone. You are good, and I call on Your name to heal my body and protect my family from sickness. Thank you for this fever that is fighting infection. I praise You because I am fearfully and wonderfully made. Thank you for this beautiful, peaceful place to rest and heal."

ENTRY TWO

I must confess, I was arrogant. Being this sick for this long has humbled me. I recognize that I was somewhat careless when I thought and spoke about this virus. Because the majority of people do recover, I assumed when/if I got it, I would be asymptomatic or just have some mild discomfort. I know I will get through this, as I am feeling much better, and compared to some people, my case is mild. (I did get a positive result.) But the arrogance of thinking that I would just breeze through this is humbling. I was helpless to it. I am doing what I can to continue to heal and fully recover, even though it's been over fifteen days. I'm resting, taking vitamin C, zinc, and D3, and drinking lots of liquids. Other than that, I've had to let my body fight it. It was a nasty fight.

As I write today, I'm asking God to reveal what He wants me to learn from this time. The first thing that comes to mind is I'm motivated to repent for my pride. Pride that I assumed this recovery would be a breeze, and while I am mostly recovered, I will confess it was rough. The seemingly never-ending fever and isolation were more debilitating than I imagined. The second is I'm thankful for my immune system, which has fought this virus for me. My body has done what God created it to do, and for that, I am very grateful. Tomorrow is Thanksgiving, and I have much to be grateful for. I'm very grateful and kind of amazed that no one else in our house got sick. I'm especially glad Carli didn't get sick as she is getting ready to deliver any day now.

Feeling better

NOVEMEBER 2020

ENTRY THREE

It's a girl! At 11:59 on Wednesday night, three weeks early, little Stevie pushed her way into this world. Evidently she wanted to be here to celebrate Thanksgiving with us. As is typical for this 2020 journey, nothing is "normal" and not much is "easy". Carli has always wanted a home birth and with Covid, it seemed like the best plan for their/our family. Naturally, laboring at home added to the drama, but with all of the restrictions in Michigan, she wanted to deliver in the comfort of home with the people she trusted and loved. At home she was able to have her midwife and her assistant, Cole, myself, her sister Mallory and her cousin Brittney. We were all here to cheer her on and assist in any way we could.

Carli's labor was text book. She had been "uncomfortable" for several days, but none of us had any idea she was this close to delivering. I will spare the gory details and protect her privacy, but I will tell you it really was a remarkable day. It started like any other day. She worked from home on her computer and sat at the kitchen counter while I made stuffing and a pie in advance for Thanksgiving.

It was a morning like every other one. Around 2:00 much to her surprise, her water broke gradually, and naturally as a first time mom she doubted that she was going into labor. And it is true that just because your water breaks, it doesn't mean labor is imminent, as some women go days. Not Carli. By 4:00 she was having what she would finally acknowledge as "real" contractions, but laboring with your first child takes a long time in most cases, so we decided to wait until Cole got home from work to mention to him that Stevie was on her way. Honestly, I encouraged Carli to wait. We thought it would be fun to see his face as she broke the news, and we all assumed it would be hours and hours before she really got down to business. Probably not the best advice I've ever given, as by the time he got home from work she was really starting to get uncomfortable. Sorry again, Cole. In hindsight we would have given you more warning in order to mentally prepare.

Carli began to experience what no one can explain to you. You must experience the pressure and the pain for yourself to understand. She stayed calm and focused, and pushed through the ever-increasing contractions like a hero. True to her birth plan, she floated in my large bath tub, surrounded by candles while listening to her "labor of love" playlist. With Cole by her side she endured and struggled and did what women have done for centuries. Only Carli was doing it at home without any pain medication. What a trooper. By 7:00 I was beginning to get concerned as her pain was increasing quickly and the midwife was two hours away.

I cannot begin to express my relief when I knew she was in her car heading our way. True to the drama of the evening, it was raining and foggy, so extra prayers were said by all. The one thing I was concerned about, among many others, was that the midwife wouldn't get here in time and we would have to deliver the baby on our own. Yikes! That thought kept me awake a few nights I must confess, but this was Carli's desire and I counted it as another opportunity to trust in the Lord and walk in peace even when I didn't feel like it.

As she labored in the tub, the evening was also bathed in prayer. Carli asked several times for someone to pray, so we took turns throughout the evening inviting Jesus into the situation. We asked for His help. We asked for protection and provision, and we thanked and praised Him. His presence was sweet and we all were aware of what a holy event this was. By the time the midwife arrived Carli was dilated to nine. Boy, that was close. After hours of intense labor, Carli moved to her bed and began to push. (Thank you internet for providing ideas on how to prepare a bed for home birth!!) I will never forget the sweetest moment I encountered during this miraculous event. She was close to delivering. She may have been pushing at this point, and Cole began to whisper a prayer into Carli's ear. As He spoke to our Heavenly Father, petitioning Him and inviting Him to be near, a hush fell in the room. It was a holy moment. It was a divine picture of love and family, and we were all privileged to be there. It was shortly after this moment that Stevie Luan made her way into this beautiful, joy-filled and often troubled, upside-down world. There was much drama in the delivery, and as a momma, it was difficult to experience this in my home without doctors and nurses and specialists close at hand. In this moment, it was just us, and I had to trust that my daughter had made the right decision for herself and her baby. I had to trust that the midwife and her assistant knew what they were doing and were trained for any complication. I had to trust the Lord would be with us, and protect her, and see us through no matter what happened, and I once again had to let go of any illusion of control I was holding on to and trust that God is holding us all tightly in the palm of His marvelous hands.

Even now as I write this almost a week after her birth, and I watch Carli and Cole struggle to get some rest without staring at Stevie nonstop as she sleeps, and actually get some rest themselves, I am reminded of the letting go and trust factor that parenthood demands. Immediately. As I finish writing today, Stevie is on a pillow on my desk in front of me with the sunlight streaming in, soaking up some much needed vitamin D to combat her jaundice. She's beautiful. Looking so much like her momma and daddy already. Her little face, and her perfect little fingers and toes... she's beautiful, and even as her grandma I feel the responsibility of caring for her, finding the balance of what is and is not my responsibility, while supporting her momma and daddy. Knowing the balance of this and living with peace requires that I lift them all up to God figuratively, like Simba in the Lion King, and say once again, "Here they are God, they're all Yours. I'll do everything I can to do my part in keeping Stevie safe and ensure she is loved, and Cole and Carli will do theirs. The rest is up to You. Here you go Father, I trust You."

Stevie, welcome to earth

December

ENTRY ONE

A young stock boy ran away from me terrified at Kroger yesterday. I can't help but marvel at the spirit of fear that has permeated our society. I was in the produce section, as was about fifty other people. There were two young men stocking the produce along with their large cart of food next to the cucumbers. Everyone had masks on, including myself, and everyone was navigating the fruit and vegetable maze with a quiet and friendly ease. And that's when it happened. Evidently I had gotten too close to this young man and he looked at me with panic in his eyes (as that was all I could see) and he literally ran away from me all the while looking at me as if to make sure I wasn't going to follow him to his perceived six feet perimeter of safety. Never mind that he ran next to other shoppers that he was now hovering next to. I was shocked. I was confused, and I said to him, "what are you doing?". He didn't have an answer. He just looked at me covered in fear.

It made me angry, but I looked at those around me who were also wondering what I had done to this young man to justify such a response, and I shrugged my shoulders and tried to smile with my eyes as I walked away and tried to act normal searching for just the right size bag of spinach. Truth be told, I was embarrassed. I felt like there was something wrong with me. I wanted to pull my mask down and smile and tell this young man and those around me that I have already had Covid. I have the antibodies and I am healthy. I wanted to tell them that I am only wearing the mask to bring them peace and help them feel safe as I was now immune. But I didn't do any of that. I knew it wouldn't matter. The culture of fear had already dug it roots down deep and my little explanation wasn't going to bring relief or change anyone's thinking.

This isn't the first time I came face-to-face with fear this week. Earlier in the week I began to notice that many of us in our home were experiencing an unusual amount of anxiety. Little Silas had a procedure detaching his tongue from the floor of his mouth and the experience was traumatizing for his thirteen-month old brain. Every time someone got near his face afterwords, he would pull away and cry. Mallory was telling me how afraid he was so we gently worked at touching his face lovingly and playfully to help him overcome his fear.

Then there were the new parents, Carli and Cole, naturally feeling stress and anxiety about their new baby girl. Was she getting enough food? How long should she sleep? What is causing her to cry or fuss? All of the questions every new parent asks themselves in the first few weeks of being a parent. But I sensed it went a little deeper than the normal watching your new baby girl breathe.

It wasn't until I was lying in bed one night thinking to myself that I would offer to watch little Stevie one night, the whole night, so they could get some really good rest. As I thought about where I would sleep and where I would put her, some horrible imaginations began to run through my mind. Fear gripped my heart as I thought about something happening to her while on my watch. That's when it occurred to me. This is Satan. I know there is no fear in love and God has not given us a spirit of fear, but of power and love and a sound, peaceful mind. This is a spirit of fear that is not from God, so I prayed and the Holy Spirit helped me to see that from the littlest one in the basement to grandma on the third floor, there was a thread of fear weaving its way through our home. AH HA! "Oh no you don't Devil!" I said to myself and I turned to Mike and explained what was happening with me and the kids and asked if he would pray with me.

As we talked about it before we prayed, I realized the common thread was the traumatic experiences we had all recently experienced. From little Silas's experience at the doctor's office, to Mallory's experience having to remain calm for her little guy when she probably wanted to cry herself. Then there was the birth that occurred under our roof. While it was a miracle and beautiful, there were also some very scary moments for both Stevie and Carli. It was definitely difficult for me to watch my daughter go through that. What I've learned about trauma is it can open a door to the enemy if we are not on guard. The fear of the moment can take root and if we do not recognize it, the roots can get all tangled up down deep and affect our hearts, sometimes for years to come.

That night we took authority over the spirit of fear. We commanded the enemy and his lies to leave our home, and we invited God's Spirit to speak truth to our hearts as we received God's amazing grace and love to cover Mike and I, our children and grandchildren. We went to bed that night with peace in our hearts and I thanked God as I fell asleep for revealing what was happening in our home.

Fear not

ENTRY TWO

When I saw the lights from the ambulance through the kitchen window I was relieved and frightened all at the same time. It's a sight you never want to see, and yet when you need it, you're grateful you are no longer alone in the panic of the moment. Either way, it's another surreal moment, not unlike the thousand others that have defined this monumental, bizarre year.

It was a night like any other, with the exception of having house guests from California visiting for a week. Cole's parents and sister came to meet baby Stevie. We had a great five days together. On the last night of their visit, we were watching a movie together when Mike whispered to me, "I don't feel right". That's never a good thing to hear. He said he was alright, but wanted me to know something was going on. A few minutes later he went outside to stand on the porch. This didn't concern me because he is an avid moon, star and water admirer. When he called me outside, I thought, as did everyone else, he was going to show me the moon over the water or a unique cloud formation, as usual, but he called me out because he was unusually hot and thought he may pass out. After cooling off, he continued to feel faint so I requested he come inside and sit down. It was then he confessed to the family what was going on. His heart was pounding in his chest and it took him a while before he could muster the courage to utter the words, "I think I may be having a heart attack".

We've had several experiences with friends and heart attacks. Some of them turned out great in the end with recovery and health following the incident. While others, well, ended tragically. Mike didn't want to be one of those though guys that doesn't say anything and then dies in his sleep. We had a friend that did that too. So, the kids called the ambulance and began to clear the area for the paramedics, while I tried to help Mike stay calm. The longer we waited the more anxious he got, and the scarier the situation became. In those moments, we called on the only one who we knew could influence our reality, Jesus. The kids prayed individually as they cleaned. They took turns at their dad's side and prayed. In the fear of the unknown, Mike asked me to pray and in those moments it was as if he and I were the only ones in the room. We quoted scripture we knew to be true and we called on the Prince of Peace to make Himself known in Mike's proverbial heart and his physical one as well. We reminded each other that he was going to be okay, and we would get through this.

Then the paramedics arrived and came in with all of their equipment and questions and it got real. They determined there could be blockage based on the results of their test so they put him on a gurney and buckled him in readying him for transport. By this time, I had my purse across my shoulder, my shoes on and my phone in hand. It was then I was informed, not sure by who, that I was not able to go with him. Another Covid-19 reality. He would have to ride to the hospital alone and go through all of the tests and waiting alone, and I would have to wait for updates as the hospital saw fit. The kids wanted me to go to the hospital and wait in the parking lot. While I understood their position, I knew that being home surrounded by my family praying would be better for all of us. I knew they wouldn't let me in, even if he wasn't doing well. They would treat him and do all they could for him. They wouldn't need me there. With the pandemic, they wouldn't allow me there. So, I trusted God to watch over him. I had to believe that when the Word of God says "He will never leave us or forsake us", He means it. He is with us in the valley of the shadow of death. So, we knew that neither of us were alone in this journey and we had to trust that what we believed, what we professed to be true time and time again, really was true.

It's always revealing when you get squeezed, what comes out. I've been on this journey long enough to know that I have control over very little. Total dependence and trust in a faithful, loving, good Father God is the rock I stand on. Every day.

DECEMBER 2020

ENTRY THREE

It's been a week since our exciting medical incident. Michael is feeling much better. It wasn't a heart attack as all of his tests came back normal. Thank God! He is following up with his family physician just to make sure, but upon further examination we're thinking it was stress and anxiety-induced. Naturally, he is not comfortable with this being the explanation. It would be easier to blame it on something physical, not something emotional/psychological that caused something physical. But there is no more shame in this house. We are done riding that ride; hiding, covering, pretending. All of us are dealing with something, and we don't always deal with it well. We all struggle and we all need each other to get through the tough times.

As we discuss what might have been going on, I asked him what he was thinking about before the episode. I have come to understand that what we believe affects what we think, and what we think about affects what we feel, and the actions we take are a result of those thoughts and feelings. Last week he said he was just watching the movie, as far as he could remember, but it's been a crazy year to say the least, and we were five days in to having company. Awesome company, but company nonetheless. And, when I say that having your daughter give birth in your home is stressful with only a midwife, when you're used to having doctors and specialists and nurses, etc. I don't think that fully articulates the experience, and dare I say, the trauma we all experienced. Add to that, he just resigned from his current job where he is rocking it out to join a company whose drug is not FDA-approved yet (He is a pharmaceutical sales representative). All of these decisions were bathed in prayer, and we continue to have peace with all of them, but that doesn't mean that the emotion of each of them and the fatigue from all of this living we are doing together doesn't add up and bite you. Evidently, conquering the fear/anxiety we were experiencing was going to require more than one prayer.

It was a wake-up call for all of us. We were confronted with our diet, exercise, rest and lifestyle choices. Upon reflection it is kind of funny, we intended to have a family meeting every month to check in with each other and discuss any issues each of us might be having. Nine months in to this family cohabitation experience, I think we've had two. As the instigator of the family meeting, may I say it's difficult to get seven people's schedule to coincide. No excuses, just being honest. Fortunately, we haven't had a lot of "issues" that needed to be discussed in a group setting. We've handled things pretty well as conflict or preferences needed to be discussed, so I never felt like we had to have a meeting. In hindsight, we all needed to meet, if just to connect and talk about the things that are happening in all of our lives.

Tonight our family "meeting" consists of a murder mystery game Mike purchased on line. We have no idea what it will consist of, but we are all dressing up like different characters, and hopefully it will work with the game. However, even if it doesn't, we'll have fun doing it anyway. It should be a lot of fun and a great way to connect and laugh after a very stressful few weeks.

I'm wearing pearls and a fur coat

ENTRY FOUR

Christmas is this Friday. I cannot believe how quickly time is flying by. The summer seemed to evaporate for all of us, but I figured that was because of the wedding, baby showers, birthday parties and everyone moving in and figuring out our new lives together. Turns out as I speak to others about this year, 2020 has had this unique dynamic of dragging on and never ending, while simultaneously feeling like it's on fast forward. I feel like Covid-19 is persisting with seemingly no end in sight. To say it is tragic and tiring all at the same time is an understatement. For those of us in Michigan, with the extended lockdowns and illogical closings, it's dragging on even more. Now is a great time to live somewhere where the sun shines all of the time in December and where restaurants, churches and other places are open safely to the public. Currently where I live the skies are gray and everything else is brown. I'm praying for snow tonight, and most likely in a few days it will all be snow-covered and dreamy, until it melts and turns gray and brown again. I am trying to manage the darkness of winter and the isolation of social distancing with grace and patience. I don't always do this well. Often, I chew on my frustration as I pass by people who will no longer look me in the eye, and if they dare to, who knows if they are smiling or if they are afraid because I've gotten too close to them. See... here I go, chewing again.

Time is passing so quickly, I walked away from writing the above section and as I come back to complete this entry, it is now Christmas Eve. I've stolen away for a few minutes before we go to church to pause and digest the day. Knowing how elusive time is, especially the good times, I want to soak it all in. I think I enjoy Christmas Eve almost as much as Christmas Day. We always get a little bit dressed up and go to church together, and then we usually go out to dinner. This year, it will be church and take-out. Still fun. But on Christmas Eve, we're all together anticipating the next morning filled with pancakes and stockings and presents and laughter and hugs and naps. I love the expectation, and all of the planning and shopping and cooking that goes along with it. Because I only work part-time, I feel like enjoying all of these tasks is a luxury. I totally understand that for those who work full-time and have to make all of the preparations with much less time, the anticipation is still fun, but much weightier to carry. I'm not sure why I feel the need to explain myself. I guess because I know that Christmas is a very difficult time for so many and I want to be sensitive to that. As I ponder that thought, I pause and pray for those who I know are having a difficult year. "God have mercy and show Yourself faithful to my friends. Help me to show them your love in a tangible way today. You know who they are." Amen.

Who knows what next Christmas will look like? I take nothing for granted, because when having children who are married and need to share themselves with other family members during the Holidays, there are no guarantees. This time of year always accentuates how precious life is. I don't want to miss a moment. Having said that, I hear the fam down in the kitchen eating and laughing and I am having FOMO. So, I'm off to see what baby has pooped or what the dog has chewed or who had a funny dream, etc. Whatever it is, I can't wait to hear about it.

Carpe diem

ENTRY FIVE

Christmas morning ended with an amazing surprise. Mallory and Jacob announced they are having another baby! I was delighted when the card in my gift said, "I know Silas and Stevie have brought you great joy and glee, How would you like to be a Grammy to THREE?! Coming August 2021". Next to it was a miniature Polaroid of Mallory holding a seven weeks sign. When I finally read it a second time and digested this amazing information, we all squealed with delight. None of us knew they were even trying, so this was a surprise to everyone.

I'm so excited for my daughter. She is such a precious, tender, amazing soul, and she has become such an amazing mom to Silas. Having your first baby, going back to work, figuring out how to sleep and clean, and enjoy the process is no easy task, and she managed it well the first time. Naturally, it was not without stress and some tears of exhaustion and frustration, but like the boss mom she is, she figured it out with Jacob by her side, and this time, I already see a peace and a confidence that understandably wasn't present with the first pregnancy. Experience can bring maturity if you'll let it. She did.

DECEMBER 2020

It is an amazing thing to watch your daughters become wives and mothers. It makes my heart full in a way I didn't anticipate. I think I am especially happy for them because neither of them had great experiences with young men. They didn't date much, and being single in a couple's world wasn't easy for either of them. They were not old by any stretch of the imagination, but compared to most of their friends, who had boyfriends in high school and got married in their early twenties, I know both of them were starting to wonder if love would ever find them. I knew they wanted someone like their daddy, and that's not easy to find, but God answers prayer, and both Mallory and Carli have sweet, considerate, handsome husbands who they not only love, but also really, really like. And, it's mutual. That may seem like an odd thing to say, but I know that is not guaranteed in any relationship.

So here we go again. Silas and this little one, we don't know the gender yet, will be approximately two years apart. It will be so fun to see Mallory begin to show and witness her life carrying this new life up close and personal. It will also be nice to be able to help her with Silas while she is pregnant and possibly when she has a newborn, if they are still living here in August. While the winter's seem long in Michigan, I'm pretty sure summer will be here before we know it, and so will baby.

It's the very last day of 2020 and it's my birthday. I'm 56 years old and I have great peace with that number. It means I've lived long enough to know a few things, but I'm still young enough to have another whole season of life yet to live, God willing. The third act as it were. Yesterday and today have been rough. Mike and I both had the blues yesterday. Neither of us knew why we were feeling "off", but when I asked him if he was feeling down, he admitted he was and I shared that I was feeling a heaviness as well. It was a very dark, gray Michigan winter day. We had the lights on all day. Later in the afternoon, we had the opportunity to reflect and we came to the conclusion that it could have been the post-Christmas blah's. You know, the letdown you often feel after a big event. Fortunately for us, we had the pleasure of getting together with some amazing new friends last night. Spending time with them and having the opportunity to pray with them at the end of our evening lifted both of our spirits. Thankfully, we went to sleep with full bellies and full hearts.

However, today I am still struggling. If I could describe what my emotions would look like if you could see them, I would say they are a tie-die mixture of joy and loneliness, gratitude and disappointment. In my experience, life is rarely one or the other. It rarely fits into a neat little box, and when you're an adult, a grandma even, and your birthday is a week after Christmas, it can sometimes feel overlooked by friends. I'm just being really honest here when I say I am struggling with a blossom of unmet expectations that oddly enough is rooted in the soil of a full heart. It's an odd looking flower. What did I really want today to look like? Breakfast in bed? Not really, we all get up at different times and I'm not a huge breakfast eater. A full day planned by my husband and kids? Not that either as recently we all just spent the day together eating out and shopping after Christmas. Maybe I was hoping to get a few phone calls from my bff's telling me how much they love and appreciate me? I must confess, that would be nice. While many have wished me a happy birthday on Facebook, which I really do appreciate, I've only received one call from any of my friends to connect on more than the thinnest superficial level, and in a year that has been extremely disconnected and isolated to say the least, I'm missing deep connection.

Instead of spending time with friends today, I got to take my mom to the doctor to get her toe looked at and then to the urgent care where we waited and waited to get her Covid test back as my sister tested positive after being with us on Christmas Day. Thank God, she tested negative! So, here I am vulnerable before you, confessing how immature and selfish of me to wrestle with giving up my day to be with her. How petty can I be? I didn't have any plans during the day today, and I still have my 85 year old momma to visit with! I know that someday I will wish I could have just one more day to drive with her, to talk with her about what is going on in her world. To learn more about her experience living alone, and dealing with the blindness that is overtaking her eyes. Someday I won't be able to hear her talk about my dad and their relationship. Every day is a treasure. I know this, but today as I sit in the middle of this, there is an undercurrent of disappointment.

For those in my family that are reading this, don't feel bad. I realize you asked me if there was anything I wanted to do on my birthday. I realize that in a few hours we will be having steak for dinner and spending time in worship and prayer, followed by playing a game or two. This was my request, and I know how great and blessed this evening will be with all of us together to bring in the New Year. And still I wrestle. I know that much of my malaise is due to the separation I have experienced from not being with my friends more during this year. I understand that each of them are all dealing with difficult circumstances in their own immediate families, and they all know that I am busy with the activities of my household. They all know I am surrounded by love and support. Once again, I know all of this, and yet I struggle to find contentment and joy on what should my special day.

Well, there you go. While it is a special day and while I am celebrated by many, it is just another day. It's a day were the bed still needs to be made. People still a need ride to the doctor. The baby still needs to be held. I get to choose today... life or death. Blessing or curses. Will I invite God into my hot mess or will I push it down and put on a plastic smile holding my disappointment in until something happens next week and I lose it? It is in this moment I go to the secret place and invite Jesus in, and ask Him to breathe on my heart by His Holy Spirit, knowing that it is His incredible love that I need today. It is His life-giving presence that I need to replace my self-focused humanity. He is the One who satisfies the longings in my soul. I wait. I breathe Him in. I repent, and I smile knowing He understands and forgives and loves me completely. Funky tie die emotional mess and all.

Happy New Year!

January

2021
ENTRY ONE

    The air is cold and the sky is gray, day after day after day. It doesn't feel like a happy New Year. Watching the news feels surreal. A conflict at the Capitol building while important proceedings are happening. People feeling like the election was stolen. People angry about people being angry. Forget about going on social media right now. I don't have the energy for any of that. In addition to that, Mike started a new job Monday, which he is excited about, but is also stressful for him. Zoom calls and the pressure of learning a new product, and meeting new people via his computer screen. It's all good, but not necessarily easy. Something I've come to realize is just because something is good, doesn't always mean it's easy, and starting any new job, even one you're excited about adds an element of anxiety to your life. But more importantly, with all of these factors swirling around us, Mallory just found out she is miscarrying her sweet little baby that was due in August. As expected, she and Jacob are devastated and so sad, and we are grieving along with them.

Yes, we know that God is good and He is in control, and we do believe that with all of our heart. With this belief also comes the truth of our reality, our hearts continue to break at the loss of this child. We do have hope that we will someday meet this precious soul, and Mallory will one day have the opportunity to hold this child, or walk and talk with him/her in heaven one day. I'm so proud of my children. They are caring for one another and sensitive to each other's individual situations, while living in this greenhouse of humanity. It's definitely not easy right now, but it is good.

And God continues to be good. I sense His presence as I hold my little granddaughter or feed lunch to my precious grandson. I sense Him as I sneak in to kiss my husband between calls or even as I put the dishes away. This is love. This is God. Loving through the tough times. Serving when you're tired. Trusting and praying even when you know you may not get the answer you desire.

My friend Linda sent me these scriptures today

in a text. It is just the reminder my heart needs. John 14:27 says, "I am leaving you a gift - peace of mind and heart. And peace I give is a gift the world cannot give. So don't be troubled or afraid." She continued with, "Don't be dejected and sad, for the joy of the Lord is your strength." Nehemiah 8:10

I know when people see the occasional picture I post about some fun thing we did, or some cool place we went to together, they have no idea about the situations we are dealing with. They don't really know the joy or the pain. None of us can. That is one of the reasons why I am writing this book. I never want my sharing of good news or bad to make anyone else feel any kind of pain or loneliness. People see us living together during this very difficult year(s) and think we are either crazy or really blessed. I know it is both. And while I don't feel obligated to post on social media, I do want to share the journey. I feel like God wants me to share this journey in a safe, authentic place where I can be totally honest with those who are interested in hearing about it. At least interested enough to open up this book and continue reading to this point.

Life is hard. Lessons, trials and pain are hard to endure, but they can be so very good. If we look to God, and continue to listen to and trust Him, He does a deep work that could never take place during the good times. As Job said, and my life is nothing like his I readily admit, but he said towards the end of his story of pain and suffering, "I had only heard about you before, but now I have seen You with my own eyes." Job 42:5

FROM THE BROKEN HEARTED

BY MALLORY INGRAM

WHEN THE UNBELIEF IS WEIGHING DOWN ON ME
WHEN THE VAPOR OF THIS LIFE IS BLINDING WHAT I SEE
I WILL TRUST IN THE GOODNESS OF THE LORD

WHEN THE WILDERNESS IS CLOSING IN AROUND ME
WHEN THE WAITING FEELS LIKE WANDERING FOR DAYS TO EVEN YEARS
I WILL TRUST IN THE GOODNESS OF THE LORD

I LIFT MY EYES TO THE HEAVENS
TO SEE THE STARS OF WHAT HE HAS PROMISED
I CLING TO THE WORDS OF MY FATHER
NO MATTER WHAT I SEE, LORD HELP MY UNBELIEF
DEATH OR LIFE, I WILL GIVE YOU ALL THE GLORY.

HALLELUJAH, YOU HOLD IT ALL IN YOUR HANDS
HALLELUJAH, YOU HOLD TIME LIKE THE SHIFTING OF SANDS.

THOUGH I MAY LOSE WHAT I HOLD DEAR,
ONE DAY IT WILL ALL BE MADE CLEAR,
BUT FOR NOW, YOU EMBRACE ME HERE.

ENTRY TWO

For years when it was just the two of us and then when our kids were little, Mike and I stayed home for New Year's Eve. We would have communion. We would pray together and take time to be alone to contemplate the previous year and to position our hearts for the next one. As we started having children and started to find our tribe, we began the tradition of going out to dinner and hanging out after. This was especially fun for me because I knew we were always going to be with our people on my birthday.

This year with Covid, and all of the restaurants closed in Michigan, we decided to stay home with the "kids" and make it a quiet night. Some of us made it to midnight, but it sure didn't feel like New Year's Eve. We waited until after midnight to see what Ryan Seacrest was up to in New York because we didn't want to be depressed watching the ball drop with no one there to see it. Even after waiting until 12:01 and wishing each other a "Happy New Year" with a hug, our dread was realized as we turned on the TV only to see the odd group of people they had on the New Year's Rockin' Eve show, or whatever they are calling it now. It was difficult to watch. "Celebrities", some easily recognizable, and others who I have no idea who they are or what they do, were trying to celebrate and act like they were having fun, when it was obvious they all were uncomfortable with themselves and their situation. Obviously, we didn't watch for long and we all headed off to bed.

Earlier in the evening we did take some time to quiet ourselves in the presence of the Lord. We lit some candles, Jacob played his guitar quietly and we talked and prayed together. We thought it would be fun to ring in the New Year spending time with the Lord like we used to. It ended up being a touching evening as several of us shared about how the year 2020 and the personal events from the year affected our lives. It was beautiful to hear my husband and kids share from their hearts. Something about the evening elicited this precious conversation that was uniquely tender and vulnerable, and frankly I felt like it was a new level of honesty and openness for us, myself included.

As the first few days in January came and went, I got back to another tradition I have honored on and off for years. I sought the Lord for a word or scripture for the year. Something from Him to hold on to in 2021. I feel like the Lord spoke two "words" to my heart. The first is Confident Heart. I was drawn to Psalm 57:7-11, "My heart is confident in You, O God! My heart is confident. No wonder I can sing Your praises! Wake up, my heart. Wake up, O lyre and harp! I will wake the dawn with my song. I will thank You, Lord, among all the people. I will sing Your praises among the nations. For Your unfailing love is high as the heavens. Your faithfulness reaches to the clouds. Be exalted, O God, above the highest heavens. May Your glory shine over all the earth." There is so much I love about this, but the heart of it, pun intended, is I can live confident because I KNOW my God. I have tasted and I have seen the goodness, the faithfulness, the magnificent love of my Heavenly Father. I can be confident, or steady, not tossed by the wind of what 2021 is already bringing. I can be peaceful when times are unsure. I can be relied upon by others and give of myself because I am not paralyzed by fear. My heart is confident, not because of me, but because of what He has done in my life. I know there will be times in this upcoming year when I will have to be fearless. When my heart has to be confident in my God, because if it isn't, I will shrink back and allow fear or worry, or who knows what, keep me from praising God and sharing His truth with others.

The other word that came a few days later is Servant. This word wasn't as fun to hear and accept, but when I felt the Holy Spirit whisper it in my spirit, I knew the Lord is calling me to a new level of servanthood. I'm not exactly sure what that is going to look like, but I know that He is calling me to be less comfortable this year and give more of my time and energy to others. I like to protect my peace, so I know this will be a process of maturing for me this year, and like I've said before, this might not be easy, but it will be good.

ENTRY THREE

I went ice skating on our lake today. Last year we purchased this house right before Christmas and Mike got me ice skates. I got him a chainsaw. Today, a year later, the sun is shining and ironically he is out trimming branches and I ventured out on the lake for the first time. Not growing up on the water, I have no idea when the ice is actually thick enough to get on it, but yesterday I saw a man skating all along the perimeter and today there are ice shanties out as well, so I felt like it was safe to venture out. The cool thing is there is no snow on the lake so I could skate as far as I wanted. I am surprised at the joy I felt while I was out there. The fresh air, my cheeks cold, the sound of the blades on the ice. Swish, swish, swish. It felt amazing to be outside, moving, in the sunshine. It was very therapeutic.

Being on skates reminded me of when I was a kid. For several years, maybe three or four, which is a long time when you're eight or nine, my friend Stacy and I would get dropped off at the roller rink in the morning and we would be there all day until six in the evening. We had lessons, practiced with a team of roller dancers, the Rolladiumettes, yes that was really our name, and then we stayed for the open session. I loved it. I could weave through the crowded floor with ease. My friends Stacy and Sandy and I would link arms and dance together around the floor under the disco ball. We had the thrill of holding hands with a boy during couples only. This was during the 70's, so any picture you have in your mind about us grooving across the floor with our feathered hair and bell bottom jeans is probably pretty accurate.

So today I was a kid again. An out of shape kid, but experiencing something new like a kid, nonetheless. I hope to get some friends to come skate with me as I felt like I was going to burst gliding across the frozen water all by myself. Maybe my hubby and kids will get in on the action. But until then, I think I will go out one more time before the sun starts to hide behind the trees. This time I will take some music with me, and maybe I will bust a little move while I'm out there, but probably not, as ice skates are very different from roller skates, and this momma does not want to fall.

Wish me luck

*ADDENDUM: I WENT BACK OUT. MIKE BROUGHT OUT THE BLUETOOTH SPEAKER AND STARTED PLAYING CHARLIE BROWN'S CHRISTMAS ALBUM, MY FAVORITE. I PRETENDED I WAS WITH SNOOPY GLIDING BY ME. IT WAS FUN SKATING AS THE SUN WAS SETTING, UNTIL I FELL FLAT ON MY BELLY IN SLOW MOTION TRYING TO DO A HOCKEY STOP, IN AN EFFORT TO IMPRESS MY HUSBAND. MISSION ACCOMPLISHED, HE WAS IMPRESSED BY MY AWKWARDNESS AND THE GRUNTING SOUND I MADE AS I HIT THE ICE.

ENTRY FOUR

Sunshine, glorious sunshine. I went to Florida with my sister last week. It was perfect timing. The walls were beginning to close in around me. Baby Stevie's cries sounded louder. The house seemed messier. Thinking of what to make for dinner was beginning to lose its joy. Who am I kidding? Thinking of what to have for dinner has never actually held joy for me. I think the isolation was getting to me and I was just experiencing the winter blahs that sometimes accompany life in Michigan. I think having restaurants and entertainment shut down month after month was adding to my frustration. I know it was. So, I will readily admit, when my sister said she was heading to Florida to possibly purchase a condo, I invited myself to accompany her. I was all in. "Here am I Lord, send me!" I couldn't let her go down all by herself to make such a big decision, now could I? What kind of sister would I be? (wink)

Turns out the weather was perfect. Each day was mostly sunny, 75 to 80 degrees. It was heaven, and just what the doctor ordered. We headed down on Friday and looked at seven condo's on Saturday, and then went back to see a few again on Sunday. It was so much fun driving around Fort Meyers looking at all of the different communities. Some had a golf course, some had swimming pools and they all had palm trees, a patio to enjoy the warm weather on and they were all covered in a blanket of blue skies. Eventually an offer was made and accepted, and we excitedly celebrated at one of the open, bustling, indoor/outdoor restaurants. Did I say it was just what the doctor ordered? It's worth stating again.

While Florida was amazing and the food was delish, and while the sun was life-giving and the sand tickled my toes, the best part about the trip was spending time with my sissy. Just her and I together for almost a week. I am very aware that the relationship between sisters can be tumultuous. It is often a relationship marinated in years of hurt and pain. I've seen it with the relationship between my daughters. They are only fifteen months apart and only one grade apart. This closeness in age often put them together in the same social circles. This, and having very different temperaments, occasionally caused friction in their relationship, and some of the pain from their past lingers on in their friendship today. I am grateful they are working on healing the wounds from their past. I see them navigating their differences as they attempt to accept and love one another better. It's often a messy and painful journey.

My sister and I are five years apart so there was no competition whatsoever. I idolized her. She was older and way cooler, and obviously had boyfriends way before I did. I always wanted to be around her as much as I possibly could. Sometimes my mom would make her let me in her room while she and her friend Becca put make-up on or talked about boys or did whatever they did that always seemed so appealing and mysterious to me. I think this only happened once or twice because if I'm recalling correctly, the moment I came in and sat on her floor, they stopped talking and they just stared at me until I eventually left. Their strategy worked as I only petitioned my mom a few times about wanting in. How mean! Right? Don't you feel sorry for me? The little sister. The tag-a-long. Somehow I never resented her for it. At least not for long. Most of the time she was good to me and because of the difference in our age, we lived very separate lives. Once we grew older, five years didn't seem like much time at all. Having homes of our own, jobs, husbands and children made it more of an even playing field. In fact, often when people find out how many years we have between us, they sometimes ask who is older. Every time this happens, I chose to believe this is a compliment for her and not a slam on me. She is beautiful and she does look amazing for her age, and I hold onto the fact I will always be younger than she is. Five. Years. Younger.

All relationships require work. All relationships have hurt and conflict and misunderstandings. It's what we do with all of it that determines the health of the individuals and ultimately the health of the relationships in our lives. After our time in Fort Meyers, we drove down to Marco Island to spend our last few days with a few of my sister's friends, who also had purchased a new condo. They were working on cleaning and updating their place and we were delighted to see it and help them clean and put on the finishing touches. I mention this because in the course of our visit, one of the friends mentioned that she is no longer speaking with her sister, and as a result, the kids (cousins) aren't able to maintain relationship either because of the rift between the moms. As I sat listening to her story about the events that caused so much damage in the family, I was screaming on the inside because it was all so avoidable. If one of you could have humbled yourself there... if one of you could have placed a healthy boundary here... if she would have chosen to forgive even when it hurts and trusted God to defend her and make it right — so many little choices that I heard as she described the situation and the subsequent decisions that followed. It made me so sad as I sat there and listened to her story sitting next to my sweet sister. I was so grateful for her in those moments. For her love, encouragement and acceptance. We've had our disagreements and opportunities for offense. That is for sure. As I sit here now, reflecting on her friend's heartbreaking situation and on our relationship, I think about the one thing that has developed healthy fruit in our relationship. The one habit that has kept us from pulling away. It's in the small moments. The small offenses. Somehow we have been able to address them. To not hold them in so they festered like a fungus. Somehow we each knew we were loved and respected by the other. We know that we are for one another and that it is the devil that wants to drive us apart, never the Lord. It is that belief system that has enabled us to have the difficult conversations or to just let the minor hurt go while assuming positive intent from the other person.

Joyce Meyer says that she has gotten to a place where she is unoffendable. She trusts God to defend her and she understands that people hurt people and as far as it concerns her, she is going to walk in the habit of living in grace and love. Covering, thinking well of and letting go of the hurts that can so easily get us stuck in bitterness. I love this and desire this for my life as well. As my sister's friend finished her story, she mentioned a list of things her sister gave her that should be included in her apology, in order for her to be able to forgive her. Let me briefly say, when God requires forgiveness it's in order set us free from needing to be the deliverer of justice and judgment. That's God's job. When we allow God to do His part, He is able to do what He does in our heart. So, should she forgive with or without a list? Yes. Was there a long list? Yes. Were there a lot of what I would consider petty things included on the list? Yes. Were the petty things petty to the one who has been holding on to them for so long? Nope. Would it take a God dose of humility and love to walk up to her door and meet all of the demands? Absolutely. But oh wouldn't it be worth it?! To reconcile and have peace in the family. To fight for relationship with one of the people in the world who knows you best. And on the flip side, the sister could be the peacemaker and rip up the list and hand the pieces to her, declaring "I forgive you. You are worth more than any of these demands." My heart ached for that to happen in their lives.

Having said all of that, I understand that there are toxic people in our families/lives that we have to protect ourselves from. The alcoholic father that has apologized for his outburst for the hundredth time or the controlling mother that has manipulated her way into your marriage once again only "trying to help". Whatever the scenario, I don't want to minimize those toxic relationships. Often, forgiving and separating with healthy boundaries is the very best thing for those involved. Sometimes it's best to forgive (not necessarily forget) while no longer allowing that abusive person access to our lives. I've had to do that as well. It's not fun.

Today I pray for those sisters. I pray for reconciliation, healing and unity. I understand that the rift in their relationship was not about the defining fight that was described to me, but about years of unresolved grievances, misunderstandings, hurt and pain. I understand that left to ourselves it's impossible to be "quick to listen, slow to speak and slow to become angry" like James 1:19 declares. 1 John 4:19 says, "We love because He first loved us". We've got to know this love in order to give this love, and as I write that statement, I realize the real secret my sister and I share. We were loved and nurtured by our parents, and we both knew Jesus at a young age. His Spirit is the Healer, the love and grace Depositor, the Heart Softener. I'm grateful for His presence in my life. I know I will have the choice today to rise up, to take the bait of offense the devil is throwing my way. I need the Spirit of God in abundance now, to speak truth to my mind and to my heart about who I am and who He is. I'm desperate for more of this revelation and for more of His presence in my life.

More Lord

JANUARY 2021

February

2021
ENTRY ONE

I've got a secret! Mallory is pregnant again. A few weeks ago I was shopping and found a little shirt for Silas to wear that said "Big Brother". I brought it home to Mal because I wanted her to know that I was praying and believing that she would get pregnant again soon. I thought it would be a fun way for her to tell us when it happened. Who knew it would happen this soon? The other day while I was still in bed drinking my coffee as I often do, she and Silas came up to visit me, as they often do. She was followed in by Carli and Stevie, and then by Mike. I wondered what this family moment was about, but we have so many family moments these days, I figured it was just another one of those days, until Mallory told me to check out his shirt. Sure enough, there it was, the big brother shirt I purchased only a few weeks ago.

What great news! What a joy and a delight. And what a surprise. It was only a month ago that she miscarried. I'm always a little bit taken back when the girls conceive so quickly, as it was not as easy for me. I struggled for years wondering if it would ever happen for me. I prayed. I begged. I ranted. I cried. I worshiped. I trusted and I struggled trusting. Then I did it all again. After three years, for some miraculous reason, it unexpectedly happened for us. It could have been the fact we were contemplating adoption. It could have been the fact that years were passing and a resolve to trust God was finally taking root. Perhaps God had worked out of us or worked in us whatever He needed to in order for us to be ready for this brood. I'm not sure, but we sure were excited.

Now that I think of it, getting pregnant with Mallory came pretty quick. I thought Carli would be my miracle baby. I didn't honestly expect more children. I was delighted to have a daughter to love and guide and enjoy. Carli was only six months old when I conceived Mallory. Having two little ones that close together was a challenge to say the least. Then Nic came along and I had three kids under the age of four. Those were wild, crazy times and now it's happening all over again. My kids are having kids, and under my roof yet. It's a joy I didn't anticipate. There's a depth to my love for them I could never manufacture on my own. It's the love you have for your children magnified and given without the daily exhaustion of parenthood.

This is a wild ride we are on. One I treasure greatly. As I'm coming to the end of this entry I hear Silas coming up the stairs looking for me again. I've got to go. He'll be sixteen in a flash, and that will be fun too.

ENTRY TWO

Both of our mothers are in the hospital. They both went in a few days ago. My momma for a racing, irregular heartbeat and Mike's mom for low hemoglobin and abdominal pain. I took my mom in and had to leave her at triage because of Covid. I hated that I couldn't make sure she was in her room all tucked in. I couldn't help her with the TV remote and show her how to work the bed. She can't see very much at all, so it's really hard for her to be in a new place. Thankfully, she said the nurses are nice and are willing to help her.

I'm sure they're used to having to be more attentive now that family members are not allowed to be with patients. I'm guessing that has made their jobs even more difficult or maybe it's better because they don't have to deal with all kinds of people needing all kinds of things. Maybe it's a little bit of both.

My sister-in-law in Indianapolis is able to go in and see my mother-in-law. I'm not sure why it's safe there and not here, but I'm glad she's not alone. Sadly, we found out today she has colon cancer. We don't know the details yet, but at eighty four that's never a good thing. She's a trooper though. She's ready to face whatever comes. Both of our mothers are. They both know and love Jesus. This bring us great peace as we navigate this trying time.

My mom has to get shocked with the paddles in the morning if her heart isn't on a regular rhythm by morning. She's scared about that, I can hear it in her voice. My mom is a very independent, strong woman, so it's very unsettling to hear her afraid. I get it though. If she's not better, they will shock her to stop her heart so it can be started again. Kind of a freaky thing. She asked me today to put a call out to friends and family so we all prayed at noon for her heart to get back to its regular beat. She wanted all of the nurses and workers to see God move. I'm trusting when we speak in the morning, she'll be out of danger and ready to get picked up to go home. That is my prayer.

Life is short. You never know what the next day will hold. I had no idea Saturday morning I would be leaving my mom in the hospital for days. We also had no idea Mike's mom would be heading toward this scary diagnosis. Every day is precious.

I have a friend who keeps a bow on her phone at night so in the morning she will be reminded that every day is a gift and to live accordingly. I love that. I understand that even more today than I did last week, and as I'm finishing up tonight, I see the lights on outside as the snow is gently falling *(Edward Scissorhands* style*)*. I see my hubby has built a fire and he and some of the kids are hanging out together enjoying the snowfall and warm fire. That's my cue. I'm off to join the freeze, I mean fun. I'm off to join the fun.

ENTRY THREE

Love is in the air. Yesterday was a really great day. In the morning I was watching Stevie because Carli and Cole got away for the night for Valentine's Day. It was their first night away from their sweet baby girl. Stevie slept great while I had her. I on the other hand didn't sleep at all. I maybe got a few hours. My body was on high alert even though Stevie sleeps great, all night! I'm just not used to being responsible for her little precious life.

In the morning, Mike and I took her out to breakfast and then we went to church with Jacob and Mallory. It was so nice to be out and about, and to be in church again. Stevie was so good. She slept for part of the service and then smiled as Mallory held her while she grunted and pooped a big pile right during the sermon. Perfect. In the afternoon, Mike and I were kicked out of the house so the kids could prepare dinner for us for Valentine's Day.

When the restaurants were all shut down for Covid, Nic gave us a "night out for dinner" gift certificate as our Christmas gift. He has always been a gift certificate giver. On Father's Day Mike has received numerous invites for 18 holes of golf and when Nic was younger, I received booklets of coupons from him with a coupon good for one hug or kiss, or for coffee out, that kind of thing. Looking back, I can see now that he is a quality time guy. All of these years I thought he just didn't like to shop. Well, it may be a little of both.

This time, Nic got everyone in on the fun. While

Mike and I went out to see a movie, the kids transformed the house into a candle-lit, flower-flooded restaurant. It was beautiful and really, really sweet. Mallory greeted us at the door behind her reception desk and asked us if we had a reservation. As she smiled in the candle light, I could see her in my mind's eye as an eight-year-old pretending, another *Father of the Bride* type moment for me. Jacob was our bartender, Carli rearranged the house to create a beautiful environment, one of her many gifts, and Cole worked in the basement along with Nic to create a yummy dinner for Mike and I.

Nic was our server, with a smile on his face and a towel draped over his arm. He spent the evening catering to our every need. He too reminded me of the little boy who used to pretend to play football in our backyard all by himself. Only he's not a little boy anymore, he's a man. A sweet, gentle, quiet thinker who still enjoys family time together, playing games or just hanging out. There were several years that were strained between us. By the time he went off to college, he was really ready to get away and venture out on his own, and we were also more than ready for him to do it. It was time. Those were rough years for all of us. We understood that the conflict was a natural part of the pulling away process. He was no longer wanting to live like we live, and he had to go out into the world to figure out what he wanted his life to look like. But being on a college campus, with all it entails, was not the best experience for him. He would tell you this himself; however, nothing is wasted and this time back home has brought great healing for all of us. He is being positioned to get back out there, this time for good. I'm so glad that we've had this time together to renew our relationship with him as a man.

Every once in a while when I get together with friends, I will get a passive comment about how adult children need to be out on their own, and trust me, I get it! The last thing I want to do is enable my kids to NOT reach their full potential. None of the people I know come out and say what we are doing is wrong, but every once in a while, I can feel a little judgment in their questions.

"So, how is Carli doing? Has she found a house yet? What is Nic up to? Is he still working at Lowe's?"

It's not all the time, but every so often I feel the pressure for them to move on. And if I'm honest, I am probably filtering their questions through my own insecurity and desire to do the right thing. I too believe when we do too much for our kids, enabling them, it communicates to them that we don't feel they are capable, and we don't believe they can make it on their own. Our goal for this time together is the exact opposite.

All of our kids have been out on their own and by

some odd wind that blew, we find ourselves together again in this big house on the lake. I know it's not forever. I know they are paying off debt that was nipping at all of their heels. They are also now positioned to save for whatever comes next. I'm delighted we've had this unique opportunity together. I never thought we'd be living this way with our adult children. I was proud that they were all out, doing their thing on their own, and sometimes I wonder what God was up to when He brought us all back together. Maybe someday we will look back and know, or maybe we won't. Either way, I'm okay with it. I'm enjoying this snow covered time of isolation together.

ENTRY FOUR

I've been watching Silas all week. I'm tired. I'm glad I had my kids when I was young. These days I like to have my down time to do whatever I want to do. This week I've been reminded of what a sacrifice it is to have children. You really give up your ability to do whatever you want, whenever you want. That's

FEBRUARY 2021

what makes being, let's say... middle-aged so great. You finally get to read that book or watch that show or eat that cookie without someone needing you to wipe their butt or fix the computer or wash their uniform, etc. It's really quite wonderful.

But this week I'm back to needing to be attentive 24/7. I haven't slept much because my body is on high alert with the responsibility of keeping this little guy alive and well while his mommy and daddy are away for a week in the Florida sunshine. It really has been a gift though. He's such a precious little guy, and while I do get to see him all of the time, there is nothing like being with him for this extended length of time. Grammy is tired today though and ready for mommy to come home. I think in other culture's where families dwell together it's probably more out of necessity. They probably can't afford to all have their own homes. But, now that we've been living this little experiment for a while now, I think other cultures are on to something. I can see how we are learning from one another and relying on one another way more than we ever would if we all lived apart. This experience watching our little guy has also created a desire to pull my mother in a little closer. She's super independent and really enjoys living alone, but as she is losing her eyesight and getting more frail, I am committed to having her over more to benefit from all of the life that resides in this house. She came over this week, just after she got out of the hospital. We didn't want her to be alone, and there was a snow storm coming, so we grabbed her for the night. It was really sweet watching her enjoy Silas. Watching her enjoy all of us. She would wander around and visit with each of us. I noticed her walking over to where Stevie was sleeping in her little pod in the dining room, and just stand there, looking at her. Thinking. Then she would make her way over to where I was unloading the dishwasher and just plop down. It was nice to have her here with no agenda. No crowd or busy activity, just being together. I truly believe we were meant for relationship. We're not meant to live life alone. We might not need to live with them, that's for sure, but we will always need people in our life to challenge us and love us and help us to see the world with greater depth and color. And with that thought, I believe Silas is up from his nap. Maybe I'll see if he wants to try to color with Grammy. He'll probably just want to eat the crayon, but who knows, we might have an artist on our hands.

Pee - yew, that's one poopy diaper

FEBRUARY 2021

ENTRY FIVE

I'm very aware today about how important consistency is. Sometimes staying consistent is more important than being exceptional. Take podcasts for example. I've thought about starting a podcast, more than once. You may have as well. A lot of people start them, but the ones that are successful are the ones that have pushed through the novelty and excitement that comes from doing something new and consistently delivered fresh content. Rain or shine, in sickness and in health. My friends Joy and Tara have done just that. They started a Bible study on Facebook Live during the Covid-19 lockdown and they never missed, a morning. Monday through Friday, 8:00 am. There they were, faithfully talking to one another about the Word of God and what He was saying to them that morning. Yes the content is grace and truth-filled and very anointed, but as I've watched their numbers grow, I know that one of the things that make them special and stand out from the rest is their faithfulness to the listeners/watchers. They currently have almost a thousand viewers every morning, month after month. And that's not even counting the thousands that watch later on Facebook and YouTube. They are dependable and that helps to make them irresistible. We all know that every weekday morning they will be there ready to share with us the truth of God that has been downloaded to them fresh that morning. Those who tune in everyday know they will hear the Word of God and be challenged to apply it to their lives. Joy and Tara's faithfulness and consistency definitely adds to their success. And to mine too.

Take this little book you are reading. I'm not an amazing writer. Okay don't get your panties in a wad. I'm not using false humility here, I'm simply making the point that there are thousands of people that write as well or even way better than I do. They are more creative and clever, and use gooder grammar. (wink) But as the winter is growing long and spring is just around the corner, I find myself getting busier with my counseling. This is a pleasant surprise, but as a result, I'm having to push through and fight the temptation to give up on this book. After all, there are people who I see every week face-to-face, and I get to experience their aha moments, and precious and holy times of healing touches from the Lord. What if I do all of this writing and no one reads it? Or, what if they read it and think... whatever. That may happen, but what I do know is if I don't consistently continue to write, no one will read it. I won't have a book, I'll just have a divine push I don't finish. I'm beginning to realize the charm of this book is the week by week, month by month consistent sharing of this journey I am on.

So, as I am getting busier than ever with everyone here in the house, adding counseling to my schedule several days a week and trying to feel inspired to write every so often, I remind myself that there is blessing in discipline. I remind myself of when God called me to this writing journey. So, I'll push through come rain or shine. In sickness and in health. And, if God has called you to do something, I hope my little entry here today encourages you to keep going. To do it even when it doesn't feel like it's doing any good.

Doin't even when I can't see it

March

2021
ENTRY ONE

Becoming a counselor has been more challenging and more rewarding than I ever imagined. I started on this journey over five or six years ago when our family was experiencing conflict and Mike and I realized we were stuck in unhealthy patterns of relating with each other and with our kids. We needed some outside help to speak truth to some areas of our life where we didn't know what we didn't know. For me, counseling led to training that was just what The Doctor ordered. We had recently left our church of twenty four years and were seeking God for healing and freedom from devastating hurt, wrong mindsets and toxic thinking.

I had just completed my first book, *Death of a Church Lady, Confessions of Hurt, Healing and Freedom*, and I was amazed how much the revelations and freedom I received by pressing into the Lord and seeking voices of truth during that heartbreaking time, were the same concepts that were later described in my training. I didn't have the language for it in the book, but the revelations I experienced in my journey to healing and freedom were also the concepts that God wanted to take me through on an even greater level through the three year process of becoming a licensed Biblical Christian Counselor.

He's good like that isn't He?! When we seek Him, we find Him. He never leaves us alone, floundering like a person in zero gravity. As we surrender to Him, pursue Him and invite the presence of His Holy Spirit to do what only He can do in our lives, it's as if He puts gravity boots on us so we can walk confidently, feet to the ground, head above butt, no longer flailing about trying to remain upright. He begins to put our lives and our priorities in right order, so some of the things that once seemed so difficult begin to happen automatically.

I have the privilege of speaking with some amazing, precious women and families. With only a couple of months under my "professional" belt, I am already amazed at what a number the enemy of our soul, satan, has done to all of our beliefs about who

God is and who we are. Lie after lie, we are confronted with the counterfeit script we have all spoken to ourselves year after year. This belief system of "I'm too much...", "I'm not enough...", "I'll never...", "God isn't...", "God doesn't...", you get the picture. These statements become our blueprint in times of great trauma, embarrassment or sometimes even in times of missing out on things we all need. Things like being cherished and understood by a parent. It sounds like a simple thing, but so many of us have never experienced what it is like to be the apple of someone's eye. Even if we didn't know we needed it at the time, we feel the emptiness, and the longing as we grow. For most of us, these lies become our truth when we are young, and for many of us, it remains the voice we continue to hear in our mind, fifty or even sixty years later. We repeat it to ourselves in stressful times until God is able to reveal it to us, and is able to speak truth to it so He can heal it. What I said in the previous sentence fits in one sentence, but can take months and even years to fully see the results of in our lives. We marinate in these beliefs and it can take years to rinse them away. God is so good to peel the layers away one by one so as not to damage us further. He is gentle and kind and always moving to bring who He is to who we are.

Today, you may feel prompted to take a moment and ask Jesus, "What lie am I believing about myself that you want to speak truth to"? If something comes to mind, trust that it is from God. Then ask Him what the truth is, and ask Him to help you replace the lie for the truth.

ENTRY TWO

We had words. Tempers flared and my heart hurt for a few days. Let me back up and say, I had an argument with someone in the house the other day. It doesn't happen very often, but once in a while, living this close together, there is bound to be some conflict. Thinking back, each of us had valid points and each of us were correct in some ways, but that didn't make the situation go away because obviously, we both thought our position was the right one. I chewed on the encounter for a few days (not always a great idea) but this time it helped because as I thought about the situation, I slowly moved from wanting to defend myself to wanting reconciliation and connection more. Naturally without dealing with the hurt, it remained a slight irritation just below the surface, so the next little offense also set me off. It was at this point I realized I had a choice. I could put my flag in the dirt and hold my ground or I could do something to meet this person heart to heart. I offered going out to dinner together to get away to relax and enjoy one another. The invitation was accepted and we had a lovely evening out last night. We ate some yummy food and walked downtown Ann Arbor and just took a breath. I'm grateful that I live with people who love me this much. People who are willing to push through the difficulties of relationship and fight for connection.

During dinner we did have a productive conversation about the topic of the argument, but when I brought it up, I did it in such a way as to listen to understand their perspective. I brought up the topic with, "I love you, are you willing to help me understand?" Something like that. What I didn't do was just bring up my perspective and what I thought about the situation, and make sure that my position was understood right away. I was able to do that in the course of the conversation, but only after I was willing to hear what they said, and after they felt cared for. I'm not tooting my own horn here, I'm 56 and I'm still learning how to relate to those around me in a healthier way.

I will admit, communicating in a non-threatening way, yet still speaking the hard truth in love, was not easy, as I am not a fan of confrontation. Some people enjoy it, I do not. But I know that having the hard conversations will take us to even a deeper connection and understanding if we will let them. When we got home from our dinner, the person and I stood out on the porch in the cold night air and looked up at the stars together. It was quiet and peaceful and one of those moments that make the difficult thing worth it. Humility had softened my heart and made room for the love of God to flow through me. As we stood there I mentioned that I didn't want my adjustment to working/counseling more to negatively affect the family. I said, "What good is it if I spend all of my time and energy helping other people heal the relationships in their lives, but begin to neglect my own?" That doesn't make sense, but I could see how easy it would be for that to happen if I didn't own it and resist it. It was in that moment I realized that God had me right where He wanted me. I had to practice what I was telling others to do. I was given the opportunity to practice what I preach every day to those I am working with.

I recently had the opportunity to speak to a group of young moms. I knew right away what the Lord wanted me to speak on. The topic of love. It's a generic and frequently talked about topic I know, but I spoke about the concept of love (God) being relational, experiential, a verb, not simply a noun. And when we seek to know the love of God more or to understand it better, we are always presented with a person to love and show grace to. Love is not just a concept to understand, but an expression to be experienced, fought for and enjoyed. You know the old saying, "Don't pray for patience, God will put someone in your life to challenge you". Well, it's the same with love. If you really want to know the love of God, you will begin to see and respond to people differently. As you are deliberate about receiving God's amazing love and are willing to be used as His vessel, watch out. Your eyes will see the beauty and the pain in the eyes of those around you. Your heart will feel things for the people you encounter in a whole new way, and the more you love and give of this great force, you get filled with more. It may be exhausting, but it's definitely worth it.

Give it a try. I dare you to ask God to fill you to the measure, overflowing with His love today. Then receive it and begin to give it away. It may start with a smile at the gas pump or a "hello there" on the sidewalk. It doesn't have to be a grand gesture, but I assure you, it will be grand.

I promise

ENTRY THREE

Our life group, small group or whatever we are calling it these days got cancelled tonight because one of the couples was near someone who had Covid this week. So, Mike and I did one of our favorite things, we went to the movies instead. We saw an average movie and had popcorn for dinner. It was amazing! We were the only people in the theater and I only saw one other family in the whole place while we were there. It is such a unique and bizarre experience. Going to the movie theatre feels like being in a movie. You know, the kind where the pandemic hits and everyone hides. It's very surreal.

Leaving the theater Mike said something, I can't even remember what it was and I started laughing. Then I laughed harder because I was laughing so much. I'm not sure if that's just a me thing, but it happens on occasion. I'm so glad I'm married to a man that I can laugh with though. A man that will say, "Sure, let's have popcorn for dinner". A man that brings me coffee and leaves me little notes telling me he loves me. It's pretty amazing to be married to your best friend, and after thirty five years this summer, still enjoy each other's company maybe even more than we did when we were young. This kind of love is unique I know, but don't get me wrong, I don't mean to brag. I know beyond a shadow of a doubt that it is by the grace of God that we are who we are. And I realize that it is His amazing love and Spirit in us that has enabled us to stay together and to lean in during the hard times, and there have been plenty of hard times.

One of the hard times was navigating the dark

world of depression together. When one partner is under the weight of it, the entire home feels it. There is a spiritual warfare that must be fought, and let me tell you, it can be exhausting. It drains you in unimaginable ways that are more than just sadness or being down. It is often accompanied by anger and isolation and long periods of silence. Not the heathiest emotions to share in a marriage. Through our battle, I have found the greatest weapon against the depression monster is love. Lots and lots of God's amazing agape love. As I write this, the words are coming to me quickly and honestly quite easily, but living it was not easy. At all. It was scary and lonely and sad. I've gotten Mike's permission to write this, because he knows the power of shame and isolation, and has also come to realize the freedom and joy that can grow when there is a safe place to get honest and get real about the darkness.

For most of our adult lives we attended a church that did not believe in professional counseling. I do not blame the church in any way for the depression, but I believe this teaching and the culture of shame that surrounded any kind of mental illness, did contribute to the delay in Mike's healing. It was literally talked about from the pulpit, that all you need is Jesus, and He is enough. While I agree that Jesus is our Healer and Defender and the Lover of our soul, oh and let's not forget Savior too. He has made us for relationship, with Him and with each other. And while the Bible is our guide to truth and the voice of God to our hearts,

He also uses people to bring love and understanding and perspective to us in times of need. I mention this because it wasn't until Mike could finally get honest with his closest people about what he was struggling with, that the healing really began. Being in an environment where vulnerability is present and it's okay to not be okay can bring great healing. It's still a process, and some days it's still a struggle, but Mike's willingness to find healing by beginning to deal with some of the issues from his past, have brought great healing to not only his life, but to others. God never wastes. He will take the broken, hurting places of our lives and redeem them for His glory. If we will let Him.

God doesn't need us to be perfect. He doesn't need us to protect His reputation. He knows that while we are living here on this earth, it isn't heaven, and because of that, there will always be a tug-of-war for our souls. He is ready and waiting to bring restoration to the hurting places of our hearts. He is not only waiting, He bids us come. He encourages us to not only confess our sins to Him, but also to one another that we may be healed, and He is pretty direct about us not forsaking the assembling of ourselves together. There is no shame in needing people. He designed us for relationship with Him and with others. He created the family so we wouldn't be alone, and He places the lonely in families so they will have a place to belong.

Tonight as I finish writing, my heart is filled with

gratitude. I'm grateful we're no longer in a culture of perfection and shame, but one where our lives can be messy and flawed and in process, because if we weren't, we wouldn't need God, and I know that I desperately need His presence in my life all day, every day.

As for the other struggles, those I'll save for another day. Tonight I am at peace and content, and I am filled with great hope for the future.

ENTRY FOUR

I had a dream the other night. It really wasn't anything special, but I did have the thought, "I wonder if there is something in here from the Lord for me?" I've learned when I am prompted to ask myself that question, I should probably spend some time asking the Lord if He wants to use it to speak to me. Now, before I go on, let me say, I am one of those people who remembers my dreams often. I can usually wake up, have a cup of coffee and tell you about the journey I took just several hours before where Julia Roberts and I are working at a furniture store and I experience panic and embarrassment over not remembering my locker combination in the break room. Or, when I'm getting ready to go on stage with my actor buddies and I haven't rehearsed or memorized my lines, and everyone else is totally fine with our lack of preparation. Fortunately for me, the play never starts in my dream so the anticipated humiliation is never realized and my love interest in the play, Greg Brady, is never the wiser.

My husband thinks it's particularly amusing that there are often celebrity appearances in my dreams. Brad Pitt, Donald Sutherland, Tina Fey, Flo from the Progressive ads, it doesn't matter. It's always random and usually pretty funny upon reflection after I'm awake. I am often doing crazy things with people I love and know well, or have never met. My dream the other night started as I was getting ready to go to a dance. It felt like I was back in high school with the excitement and anticipation of getting all dressed up and hopefully dancing the night away with friends and maybe even a cute guy. Could be Mike, a guy I went to church with twenty years ago who's name I can't remember or Clooney, you just never know. There we're no specific people in this dream; however, I just knew I was with people I do life with and we were all moving around doing whatever it is you do when you're getting dressed up. I was frustrated as I looked for something to wear. I knew I had a dress somewhere, but I couldn't seem to find it. As I was continuing to get ready someone came in to the house and asked me to move my car. I'm not sure the reason for this, but I was happy to oblige. I grabbed my keys and headed out half-dressed. As I climbed way up into my vehicle, I realized it was a tractor trailer. As I looked up to find my way out I had to drive over the yard, which was all tore up like a construction sight. I got the rig moving and barely missed a large pile of dirt and a hole just next to it as I made a circle in the yard, ending up back where I started from. Weird right? There is nothing that stands out to me that is a spiritual lesson, but the question that kept coming to my mind is, why was my vehicle an eighteen wheeler? Why was it so big and scary to drive?

As I placed this question before the Lord I heard Him say, "You sure are carrying a lot around in that thing". He was right. It was heavy and cumbersome and difficult to maneuver, and in that moment I understood the weight of all of the people and responsibilities I am currently carrying. Wow. And not only that, but this heavy load is potentially keeping me from the joy found in the dance that is my life. So, what is the heavy load I am carrying?

Well now, let me think. It could be my kids, their need to find homes in a market where there literally are no homes for sale in their price range, and even the ones out of their price range have twenty offers the day it hits the market. These sellers are getting way over their asking price because of the great demand for homes in our area right now. It could also be the jobs they are struggling with or struggling to find. It could be any number of things that I think about during the day. Then I remind myself to ask, what is God's responsibility, what is other people's responsibility and finally, what are my responsibilities? While it's natural for me to be concerned for all of the lives living under my roof right now, I know that they are all smart, talented, hardworking people. They are kind and sweet and faithful to their friends and to one another.

So today, I "consider the lilies of the field and how they grow. They don't work or make their own clothing, yet even Solomon in all of his glory was not dressed as beautifully as they are. And if God cares so wonderfully for wildflowers that are here today and thrown into the fire tomorrow, He will certainly care for you (me). Why do you (I) have so little faith?" Matthew 6:26 and Matthew 6:33-34 says, "Seek first the Kingdom of God above all else, and live righteously, and He will give you everything you need, so don't worry about tomorrow." I am reminded by my silly dream to climb out of the cab of the big rig I am unconsciously driving, and trust in my good, good Father. Then I can take a moment to rest, to go for a walk and maybe even to do a little dance, knowing He's got me. He's got all of us. I seek Him today. To know Him and to experience His presence in my life today. My heart's desire is to continue to love Him and to love those He puts in my path well. The homes, the jobs, the relationships, etc. are His. All His. What's in your tractor trailer? If we were to open up the back and look inside, what would we see? What is the heavy load you are trying so hard to carry on your own? Perhaps it's pain from your past. People who hurt you or abused you, causing you to carry a load of grief, unforgiveness or resentment. It's heavy and it's time to let it go, again, to God. It could be the financial fear that is chasing you at night. How, where or even can you catch up?

Maybe, just maybe, the load you are carrying is not even your load to carry. Maybe you're trying to protect or help someone you love, but in doing so you prevent them from feeling the weight and making a change for themselves. Maybe. Whatever the case, I am glad for the nudge to release my cares and my worries to God, causing me to remember and know that He sees me, loves me and is working all things together for my good.

MARCH 2021

April

2021
ENTRY ONE

Today is Good Friday. I've often wondered why we call the day that Jesus, our precious Lord and Savior, was tortured and murdered, good. Intellectually, I understand why. He willingly gave Himself up, surrendering His life so that we could have eternal life with Him. That truth is more than good, but why don't we call it Sacrifice Friday, Salvation Friday, Surrender Friday or Change the World as we Know it Friday? Good Friday just seems too simple for all that it represents.

I'm reminded today of an old favorite song of mine from childhood, *He Could have Called Ten Thousand Angels,* by surprisingly to me, Loretta Lynn. The chorus says, "He could have called, ten thousand angels to destroy the world and set him free. He could have called ten thousand angels but he died alone for you and me." I remember sitting in church as a child contemplating and picturing in my mind what that might look like. What if He did call down heaven and say, "Enough?" What would that have looked like. I kind of like imagining it because I wish for His sake, He could have done it. That would have shown them. That would teach them to mock and not believe He was who He said He was. In my mind, that sure would have felt good for the moment. But my God is always about the big picture. He is always about the end game and understands the beauty of temporary pain if it achieves a marvelous goal.

In the end, He did show them. Darkness fell across the land during mid-day as if it were night. The curtain in the temple was torn from top to bottom, giving access to all. That in itself is crazy amazing, but there were also the saints who awoke from their graves to testify of this monumental event. All of those things were spectacular, but I find what Jesus did and didn't do during that Good Friday even more amazing. What did He do after hours and hours of betrayal, humiliation and torture? He forgave them all. He said, "Father forgive them, for they do not know what they are doing." What?! Forgive them? How about instead, God drops one of His life, love and power-filled tear drops on them all causing the whole area to get blown away like Hiroshima. Yeah, that sounds good to me. Or, better yet, my favorite fantasy, Jesus speaks one word and ten thousand angels, majestic with swords and lightning, come down from heaven and lower Him from the cross healed and restored, and every human for a thousand miles fall to their knees in worship to Jesus, our Savior King. Yeah, that's more like it.

But as we all know, that's not the story. As usual, He had the end game in mind. He knew He had to die. That is why He came. He offered Himself willingly to be the sacrifice for us, and He did it all with all of the grace, love and mercy He does everything with. He modeled for us in that moment the power of forgiveness and perspective, and He displayed the kind of love that can only come from the Father, Son and Holy Spirit.

One day every knee will bow and every tongue will confess that Jesus is Lord to the glory of the Father. I'm really looking forward to that day, but until that magnificent day, I will bow my knee here and now, and surrender my heart with gratitude for who He is in my life and for the sacrifice He made and the example He gave me and all of us. And I humbly acknowledge that I am included in the crowd that demanded His death. I sure don't like to think about that, but I can embrace that truth because it reminds me that I was the guilty one. He did it for me. Yes, He could have called ten thousand angels, but He died alone, for you and for me.

APRIL 2021

ENTRY TWO

Easter Sunday was such a nice day. The weather was beautiful, and if you live in Michigan, you know that it could be sleeting or freezing or gray on Easter. Yesterday was gorgeous and sunny and warm, and I enjoyed every minute of it. We started our day by going to church. I was so happy to put on my soft yellow suede jacket and even wear a little heel with my jeans. Sounds superficial I know, but day after day of sweatshirts, jeans and slippers gets old after a while, but more than that though, it was so nice to go to church with my family. Mallory and Jacob were singing so I got Mr. Silas up and got him dressed and ready for church so he could go with Papa and I. He's such a little adorable man. He is sweet and tenderhearted just like his momma and daddy. As he walked into church holding our hands in his new big boy shoes, I was flooded with joy. Look at this little guy. So precious and little and yet such a big boy. No longer a baby. After dropping him off at class we were met by Carli, Cole and sweet little baby Stevie in her peach bonnet and lace-trimmed dress. She sat on my lap during worship, and as I listened to the choir sing Hallelujah, He is risen, Jesus Christ is King... I could hardly hold back my tears.

There is nothing like corporate worship. The reality of walking into a room with like-minded people who are all there to sing about the goodness of God and worship Him together in a place where the Word of God is treasured and spoken. It's special, and I don't take it for granted any longer. I know many people who are not comfortable going back to church yet. For those who are health-compromised, I get it. There is wisdom in protecting yourself when you are vulnerable. For those who are afraid, I'm sad. I had an acquaintance reach out to me today asking if I felt it was safe to go to church as she was afraid to go. She was asking for my advice, so I shared with her that as soon as the doors were open, I was there. I shared with her that my theory is if I can go to the grocery store and be around so many people, and go to restaurants and all of the other places we go in our everyday lives, why is church any different? For me, I feel like church is more important than Home Depot or Costco. I'm not sure why it has been treated so differently.

This is not intended to be a political point. Please hear that. It is to declare the importance of faith and the value of corporate worship. I love my quiet time with the Lord. It is the connection that fuels and feeds my life, and I will probably talk about the way the Lord spoke to me during my time with Him in the next few entries, but for today, I'm grateful for the opportunity to go to church with my kids and grandkids to celebrate our Risen Savior. I'm grateful to come home and eat ham and potatoes and watch the little ones hunt for Easter eggs. I love all of the traditions we have together. These moments we have to worship and do life together are a treasure.

ENTRY THREE

This morning on their Facebook Bible study at Barn 45 my friends Joy and Tara talked about confidence and how if the devil can steal our confidence, he's got our identity. Wow! What a divine connection. The scripture they were pondering was James 5:12, "But most of all my brothers and sisters, never take an oath, by heaven or by earth or anything else, just say a simple yes or no, so that you will not sin and be condemned," As they always do, they looked deeper into why we feel the need to justify our "no" with a long drawn out explanation, justifying ourselves along the way. Their conclusion, it's a confidence problem. What if people don't understand us, like us or think whatever about us? If we are insecure about who we are and what we are called to do, we will manipulate people's perspective and do our best to make sure that everyone is okay with what we are doing.

There have been times in my life when not only did I need to justify and explain myself for saying "no", but I can recall times when I couldn't say "no" at all. I would put a spiritual face on it and say I would pray about it, and I would, but my initial response was "no", and that felt like too strong of an answer for me to give. Because of the work I am currently doing, I understand this isn't just a problem I deal with. It is epidemic. The need to be liked superseding our need to be honest and true to our self. Which gets us back to Joy and Tara's point. When we know who we are and what God has called us to do, we can relax. We can be honest with ourselves and with others. We can make Spirit-led decisions knowing that not everyone is going to like them. Not everyone is going to understand. When we live fully accepted by Jesus and are living with a fresh dose of His love daily, we are able to continue living with decisions that others don't agree with or understand. We can be okay when others are not okay.

This is a concept that has been a work in progress for me. Little by little, each decision and conversation where there may be disappointment or conflict is an opportunity for me to work this people-pleasing muscle out of my life. I so appreciate how Jesus takes so much time in John 15 telling us to abide in Him. He gives us the analogy, He is the vine and we are the branches.

In order to survive and thrive, we need to remain in Him. To remain means to never leave. To maintain that place of love, belonging and acceptance in Him first. If we don't go there first and receive those things from our relationship with Him, we cannot resist the need to get it from people. And if we get our love, belonging and acceptance from people, we will feel compelled to please those people, while never being satisfied.

I realize as I write, this is a simple concept, but that does not mean that it is always easy. But it is getting easier. Each day I have the opportunity to choose to receive the spiritual and soul-filling nutrients from my Father in heaven. When I have this posture, I have more than enough to go around, and I have the ability to say "yes" to what I feel I should say "yes" to, and I also have the confidence to say "no" to what I should decline. When I skip that place of rest and identity, abiding in the vine, and go to my hubby, kids, friends, refrigerator, television, etc. to fill me up, I lose perspective and it's harder to make honest decisions. Often, my emotions are the indicator. If I'm impatient, easily frustrated or down in the dumps, I know it's time to plug in and get a recharge from the Lord.

ENTRY FOUR

I just got back from a missions trip. I've been on many mission trips all around the world. I've had the privilege of serving and loving on orphans in India, Egypt and Haiti, sharing the love of God.

I've been on all of these trips without my better half. When it comes to leaving home for a week or more we found it is easier if one of us stayed home with the kids while the other one went, but I've always wanted to partner with Mike on a God-sized trip. This past weekend, my wish came true, and I will admit, it was harder than any other trip by far. Mike and I traveled down to his hometown, Big Stone Gap, Virginia to empty his precious mom's house who was just diagnosed with Stage IV cancer. She lived in the same house for over twenty years and as most of us, gathered a lot of clothes and treasures along the way.

We've taken many trips to BSG throughout the years. My first trip was when we were dating or engaged. I can't exactly remember. Mike had mentioned that his mother's house was near a train track, but until you are lying in your bed at night and hear that whistle blow and the charging of the wheels coming down the track 50 feet away from the house, you are certain it's the end, and we're all going to die. But somehow you survive the passing of the train and learn that it's not going to explode into the house. It just sounds like it is. When the kids were young, we investigated the tracks and they loved to put pennies on the track and hunt for the flattened remains later. Don't tell the government we did this. After years of hearing it roll on by as we sat on the front porch or were eating dinner, it becomes a sound you love. The sound of home.

Seasons change and for Gaphina (Ja-pi-na), Mike's momma, this season of independence is painfully over. Because of her cancer, she has moved in with Mike's sister Cindy and her hubby Jeff in Indianapolis and as you can imagine, this has been an adjustment for everyone. What do we do when something dear to us comes to an end and we are forced to adjust and transition to something new? We are definitely presented with a choice aren't we? Anger and/or frustration, sadness for the loss of routine and the familiar, grief, and finally sweet resolve that God is faithful and we can trust that He has us covered and will provide good things in this season as well. I have witnessed this in my own life and especially in the lives of our parents as they have aged. For my sweet hubby and I, we were tangibly confronted with this truth again last weekend.

He and I alone had three days to sweep through his momma's filled-to-the-brim home, finding a place for all of her remaining possessions, making it ready to sell. Fortunately for us, we make a great team. In this situation, he was nostalgic and cautious and I was task-oriented while making every effort to be respectful. The task was daunting and emotional, but we tackled it together. Ten hour days of non-stop evaluating, saving, giving items away to those who could use it, and tossing so many precious valuable cherished memories. But we had to do it. We had to make the hard choices. So, we opened up the doors and windows and let the fresh air in. We played our favorite set lists as a background for the journey, and we made every effort to hug once every few hours to pause and feel and connect. It was a painful and beautiful experience for me to have this precious experience with my husband, the man I love and cherish most in this world. What an honor it was to work side by side with him, doing the hard thing.

With the Explorer filled to the top with every precious item we could save, we pulled away from the land where my husband grew to become the man I know and love. The mountains and the people are beautiful there, and we hold them both deep in our hearts hoping to someday return to see them in person once again.

This trip with a mission was exhausting. The most physically and emotionally grueling trip yet, but I will cherish it forever, as with all mission trips, it's not as much about what we do while we are there but it's about sharing the love of Christ Jesus as we do it. I felt His presence the whole time we were there. It was

APRIL 2021

Holy Ground.

Next weekend we will all travel to Indy to celebrate Gaphina's 85th birthday. We will celebrate her with cake and gifts, hugs and laughter, and each of us will quietly grieve as this birthday may be her last. Pausing as I write to let this truth sink in, I am reminded once again that none of us are promised tomorrow. Each day is precious, so I'm motivated not to waste one day.

Starting with today

ENTRY FIVE

In my time with the Lord this morning He made it very clear that He is with me. I was lead to Zephaniah 3:17 where it says, "For the Lord your God is living among you. He is a mighty savior. He will take delight in you with gladness. With His love, He will calm all your fears. He will rejoice over you with joyful songs." Boy, this scripture is loaded with yummy truth. I love the imagery of God, the Creator of the universe rejoicing, dancing over me with songs of love filled with joy. That is hard to wrap my brain around, but as I think about how I adore my children and grandchildren, I get a glimpse of what it must be like. The truth from this scripture that jumped off the page this morning was that He is literally living among us. I know that this is accomplished through His Holy Spirit that resides within each of us as believers, but I love the thought that He not only lives in us, but lives among us.

When I open my Bible to Zephaniah three, I also see on the opposite page Haggai 1:13, "... I am with you says the Lord." And 2:4, "... for I am with you, says the Lord of Heaven's Armies." I love the way Father God speaks to my heart. He can take words written thousands of years ago, and speak truth to my heart today. Our home has been full of emotions lately, especially with going to Nana's (Gaphina's) 85th birthday celebration this past weekend. We were all confronted with the reality that the group picture we took with all of us there surrounding her may be the last picture we will take with her. It's a daunting thought. Naturally, we all have other life issues we are dealing with. Each of our kids are praying about and planning for their exit strategy. New homes, moving to different states possibly, the potential for different jobs, additional kids on the way and daycare costs, etc. Each of us together have a bouquet of life issues and stresses. I didn't even know what my heart needed today as I went to His Word, but as I absorb this truth of God living among us here in our house on the lake, I am comforted, and I am reminded to rest in this truth.

Peace. I can rest in my spirit and have peace in my mind and heart knowing that my Father in heaven is intimately aware of all of our needs because He is living here among us. When we are laughing around the dinner table, He is there. When we are rocking a baby to sleep, He is there as well, enjoying the rosy cheeks and chubby fingers right along with us. When we are frustrated with one another and needing to be understood and valued, He is there too, living among us. Helping us to connect in His love. He cares if we are wounded or tired or sad. He is in the middle of it all. As I meditate on this wonderful truth, I am comforted and filled again with confidence that He is good and He has got us.

I am reminded of the scripture He gave me back in January for this year. Psalm 57:7-11 "My heart is confident in You, O God; My heart is confident..." My confidence comes from above. Like the Proverbs 31 woman, I can laugh at the future because I know who holds my future. I don't know what's going to happen tomorrow. Heck, I don't know what's going to happen this afternoon, but that's okay because I won't be alone when it comes, whatever it is. The great news is, this is also true for you today. God dwells in and among His people. He sees you today. He loves you today, just like He did yesterday and will tomorrow. He has not forgotten about you. How could He when He is dwelling with you? Have confidence today and rest in His peace, trusting that neither of us are alone. Remember, He is with us.

ENTRY SIX

Boy oh boy, if you don't think the weather affects your mood, after today I would have to strongly disagree. It was 78 degrees and partly sunny... and I loved it. I started my day off on the porch with my Bible, coffee and a beautiful multicolored sky. This is my favorite place to meet with God during the spring, summer and early fall.

During the winter I have to get creative steeling away somewhere in the house, but this morning winter was nowhere to be found, and I drank in the sounds of the lake. The stillness of the air, the quiet of country interrupted by an occasional frog or bird or dog barking in the distance. I couldn't help but smile as several geese flew overhead. As they honked constantly to one another flying perfectly spaced apart, the pitch of their call changed as they approached the house and then continued overhead. It reminded me of an ambulance in England from an old movie the way you hear it coming and then it changes as it speeds on by.

Something happened out in the lake, I'm not sure what. Maybe a fish jumped up out of the water. When I looked up from my reading, I noticed how beautiful the water was, smooth as glass, with the exception of several rings of tiny waves traveling toward the shore. The ripple effect. I've thought about and spoke of this concept many times the past several years. I've noticed as I've pursued healing and freedom in my own life and then worked to begin to help others find their's. No one lives alone. What I mean is, we all affect each other, either in positive or negative ways. Our actions have consequences and those consequences always effect those around us, just like the large circle created in the lake from one small fish or bird.

Years ago, as I began talking to a counselor and allowed her along with several other influential people in my life to ask me tough questions and teach me more about why we do what we do, I began to understand the lies I was believing about myself, God and others. In that process of questioning and reflecting and getting more honest with myself, I gained perspective and understanding about my life. This shift in beliefs about myself, others and God's ways, helped me and I began to relate to others with greater vulnerability, and it created space for those around me to do the same. The ripple effect.

Likewise, I've better understood the unhealthy choices I've made that have caused those in my life to either take advantage of me, or pull away from me, or believe a lie right along with me. A ripple effect I wish I could change. But I've learned not to despair, because I've realized the immense power of grace. God's grace partnered with a humble heart can change a relationship and/or a family in a miraculous way. I've experienced it personally and witnessed it in others. It's a beautiful thing. I challenge you to try it sometime. If you've lost someone dear to you, gotten divorced or you deal with a history of abuse, and you have denied the grieving process to take place because you've been too busy feeling ashamed, angry, hurt or bitter. Go for a walk with God or a trusted friend, and begin to talk about what happened to your heart. As you acknowledge the truth about your life, right where it is, with all of the pain and the regret, whatever it might be, invite the gentle Holy Spirit to touch that devastated place. This invitation brings to light what has been in darkness. It begins to peel away the shame that has clung on from the moment of your experience. This allows the healing process to begin.

A woman I recently spoke with was devastated by divorce after her husband left her for another woman.

After years went by, she couldn't figure out why she struggled getting close to her second husband, a wonderful Christian man. As we spoke, the pain from the rejection and betrayal of her past was holding her hostage. I asked her if she had ever allowed herself to grieve the loss of her first marriage. She really didn't know. It all happened so fast and it was so tragic, and then she had to shift into survival mode in order to survive. This left little time or energy for grief, but it was sad, and she did need to let herself realize the pain it caused, not only to herself but the many people that surrounded her, especially her children. Ripple effect.

The beautiful thing is, once she began to grieve, she then was able to finally open up to her children about her pain. This allowed them to begin to grieve themselves, as they no longer needed to protect her by being strong and needing everyone to be okay. The ripple effect of restoration, vulnerability and healing was a beautiful thing to see. It's a process that is for sure. I still experience God bringing up another little lie I believe or emotion I'm not ready to deal with, and He lovingly waits for me to hand it to Him so He can do what only He can do and make beauty from the ashes of my life.

May

2021
ENTRY ONE

We are having what I can only call a full circle moment. Today we purchased the pontoon boat from our friends, John and Lisa. They were our neighbors before we moved, and they are the friends we borrowed the boat from the day we went out on the lake almost a year and a half ago. After a long, cold winter, when the sun started warming the earth, we started looking to see what kind of used boats were available. Coincidently, we had John and Lisa over for a bonfire. They mentioned their frustration with the lake they were keeping their boat on. The water is too low to put their boat in and it may be months before they can use their boat, and weeds are overtaking the lake with no end in sight. So, we offered to "take it off their hands" — for a fair price of course. Much to our delight and surprise, they agreed.

Our boat arrives next week and I'm excited! All of last year we were not able to get out on the water we admired from our porch everyday, with the exception of a little broken down fishing boat my brother gave my son. I am grateful for the short amount of time that motor worked so we could at least see the other homes on the lake from the front. With all of our finances going to the renovation our home and finishing our basement for our kids to live in, getting a loan for a boat just didn't seem prudent (Thank you Dave Ramsey). After a long winter, we are positioned to make that dream a reality.

I'm looking forward to the change in perspective. What is it like in the middle of the lake? How does jumping into and swimming in the deep water compare to wading out into the water navigating the weeds and fish and stones. All of the little pleasures of lake living (wink). I'm looking forward to discovering new places to rest and play and spend time with friends and loved ones. I'm looking forward to taking my coffee, Bible and notebook, my Spotify playlist and spending some time with the Lord out on the water. As I've learned from past experience, good conversations happen out on the water. The breeze, the sun, the rhythm of the boat... it's special.

I'm grateful for something fun to look forward to. In a weird way, I'm glad we waited to get a boat. It certainly helps me to appreciate it more now. As I pause and reflect about the goodness of God in my life, I'm grateful that I have people in my life to share it all with. Very grateful.

ENTRY TWO

It's quiet in the house this week. Carli, Cole and little Stevie are in California for a little visit. They went to celebrate Mother's Day with Cole's momma and for Carli to be in the sunshine and palm trees for Mother's Day and her birthday. I'm happy for them. It's been a long hard winter for the newlyweds and they've handled it all really well.

While they are gone, Mallory, Jacob and Silas are headed up north for a long weekend away. They also need some time to spend with friends and get a change of scenery. They are vacationing with a few other families who also have small children. I watched them load up the explorer with portable cribs, strollers, backpacks and all of the extras you need when traveling with little ones. I remember those days well. I am also happy they are taking some time to rest and relax together.

We've always placed a high value on spending time together with our kids in a different location. Home gets tedious with all of the cooking and cleaning, homework and e-mails, etc. We have some amazing memories traveling as a family. Most of them are captured on film and are gathering dust in photo albums in my basement storage room. Through all of the moves, I couldn't let any of those boxes go. They are too fun to look through every once in a while. They are a tangible reminder of the life we have shared, but more important than the pictures I store in the basement (or post on social media), are the memories I hold dear in my heart that we have created together.

First, there are the trips up north to Traverse City or Mackinac Island. We started this tradition when the kids were still small. The beach, the merry-go-round in the mall, Shirley Temples at the top of the Grand Traverse Resort, riding bikes around the island, etc. We usually had to get sweatshirts because somehow it always turned out to be colder than we anticipated, but the hunt for just the right one was part of the fun.

We took a trip to NYC when the girls were in high school. This was perfectly situated in the middle of my designer purse phase. Somehow, perhaps in my quest for a deal, we found ourselves in a back alley, up the stairs in a dark building, led into a small room full of counterfeit purses by a man we had never met before. As we moved further and further into this building, Mike and I looked at each other, and with just a glance we agreed, "Are we crazy? He could be taking us somewhere to murder all of us, and no one would even know we were here". Thankfully, we returned to the light of the street safe and sound. I probably saved a total of $20 as a result of our terrifying journey, and when it comes up, I remind Mike that we wouldn't have that *fun* memory if it weren't for me and my passion for a new Michael Kors handbag.

Our all-time favorite vacation was our crazy trip out west in a rented RV. Yes, I scheduled our itinerary with no idea what I was doing. Yes, we raced from one KOA campsite to another with barely enough time to enjoy, anything. Yes, the kids fought over the laptop. Yes, the air conditioner was broken and we didn't have time to stop and get it fixed because of our KOA reservations, so it was noisy and our hair was in knots all of the time from the wind whipping around in the cab. Yes, I ended up in the emergency room in Provo Utah from dehydration as a result of our one bottle of water hike in Moab. I could go on. But we also made a home movie in the cornfields of Kansas, and we played for a day in God's sandcastles at the Garden of the God's in Colorado Springs. We rode horses and had dinner around the campfire at a dude ranch in the mountains of Montana. We made it home in one piece with an amazing experience that we will all laugh about and treasure in our hearts forever.

So, while the house is quiet, I ponder these precious memories and I am confronted with the truth that this amazing time we are having together in the house on the lake will join this amazing montage of memories in my mind. I am at peace knowing that every day is a gift. Knowing this, I will enjoy the peace and quiet knowing the energy and noise that accompanies our crew will return soon.

But for now, a nap

ENTRY THREE

I've been reading 1 Samuel the past several mornings. I've read it many times, and somehow, it's always fresh. This time as I read about the children of Israel and how they pined for a king, like all of the surrounding kingdoms, I am reminded of how we do that too. We are citizens of heaven and yet we live like this world is our permanent home. So often, we let what we see with our natural eyes dictate our choices. It makes sense, it's harder to walk by faith than it is to walk by sight, so often we embrace a temporary mindset.

Reading about Israel's first king, Saul, sometimes I can really relate to this guy. When they were looking to crown him king, they found him hiding in the baggage. How ironic is that?! His "baggage" of the fear of what others thought about him consumed him, and was holding him back from receiving his rightful place as king. This was his weakness and ultimately became his downfall — the fear of what other's thought about him. Me too Saul. I get it. I also have lived much of my life avoiding failure. Wondering, what will people think? Who are these all important people that I have allowed to slow me down? Honestly, a few naysayers do come to mind, but that's on me, not them. God never told me to give them that power. On the contrary, 1 Thessalonians 2:4 says, "For we speak as messengers approved by God to be entrusted with the Good News. Our purpose is to please God, not people. He alone examines the motives of our hearts".

As I write this, I realize the progress I am making in this area. Who will want to read this book? Why is my life worth reading about? Who do you think you are? It's getting so old. Honestly, I'm over it. I am living my life, doing what God calls me to do with confidence and joy. And if anyone thinks I'm arrogant or trying to be famous, I will direct you back to 1 Thessalonians 2:4.

I know I'm not. I know it is by God's grace I stand free and loved. I also understand that it is in humility that we find peace, joy and promotion.

Back to 1 Samuel. As I think about Israel's kings, I can't help but compare Saul with David. He was the shepherd boy made king. This guy knew who he was and didn't need anyone to approve of him. He received his identity from God and it was from this relationship that everything in his life flowed. In 1 Samuel 13:14, God tells Saul through Samuel that the kingdom is being taken away from him and given to "a man after His own heart". We've heard this phrase a lot. I've prayed that I too would be a woman after God's own heart many times, but today, as I was pondering this truth I felt like the Spirit of God tweaked this perspective in my understanding.

I've always thought that David being a man after God's own heart meant he was in agreement with the things God agrees with. That he cared about the things that God cares about. But today, the thought took a little turn and I realized that while those things are true, it also means that David was after His heart. Seeking God, desiring God, after God... His affection, His presence, pursuing Him. Not just resembling His heart, but pursuing His heart.

I've spent a lot of time running alongside God. Running after the things He is running after. Serving Him, obeying Him. Seeking to understand Him and think like Him. Maybe it's time I pivot and run into His heart and rest a while. Maybe that was David's secret. He was after God, period. From that place, I'll call it knowing/relationship, he was able to soothe Saul's tormented spirit and take down Goliath, the Philistine giant. He was able to endure hardship while maintaining faith and perspective. He could lament and cry out to God honestly because God's love was a reality in his life.

I want to not only have a heart for the things that Father God has a heart for, but more importantly, I want to have a heart for Him alone. No fear of man. No fear of the future. Just Him. His loving, safe heart.

MAY 2021

June

2021
ENTRY ONE

    I knew this day would come. One of the exit strategies is coming to fruition. Carli and Cole will be the first to leave this crazy experiment of ours. They are going to head back to California in July. Cole is going to pursue some more schooling for a new adventure he is embarking on, and Carli is looking forward to reconnecting with some longtime friends back in the sunshine under the palm trees where she belongs.

    They came to live with us this time last year. The journey has been quite eventful for them and for us. We've navigated many relational situations in the past year, and I'm so glad that our hearts are even closer at the end of the year than they were at the beginning.

There was great potential for this not to happen. As you can imagine, living together as adults can bring some sticky situations. We had disagreements, and we had awkward situations, and each time we were presented with the choice of how to handle them and how to respond to each other. I can honestly say that humility and the passion for heart connection kept us from driving each other crazy and ending our time together with frustration and/or resentment.

As I look back, I realize we were able to do this because of the healing and freedom God has brought to our lives in the past several years. In one of the darkest times of my life, I was pursuing truth and healing and God lead me to a Codependent Workshop. This workshop was the catalyst, ushering in everything I am doing now. Writing, counseling, and next week I will lead this same workshop throughout this summer. It's another full circle moment for me.

Stephanie Tucker describes codependency this way, "it is essentially all the fruits that arise in our lives when we are lacking God dependence. We either erect a system based on being led by the Spirit, or a system based on trying to 'do' Christianity in our own strength. The tricky thing is that at first they can look quite similar". The fruits of peacekeeping, people pleasing, controlling and/or fixing people or situations are just a few of the bitter fruits that have grown in our home.

But, you don't know what you don't know. I didn't know why I needed everyone to be okay. Why I avoided painful situations and oftentimes didn't get honest because I knew it would cause conflict in a relationship. Now I value tough times and tough conversations, and sometimes the pain we endure as a result. I value it for the humility is brings. For the precious opportunity to rely on God to move on my behalf, or on behalf of a loved one. I know now that the relationship will be deeper, richer on the other side of vulnerability, heart connection and understanding. I value the maturity that comes from perseverance and endurance.

I used to be uncomfortable praying to Father God. I always prayed to Jesus. There isn't anything wrong with that, but the Word of God teaches us to pray to our Heavenly Father and I just wasn't comfortable doing that, until I was. Many years ago, during an inner healing/freedom ministry leadership seminar, I was taken through an exercise. I was instructed to close my eyes and picture God. In my mind's eye I pictured Him far away, up a marble staircase, seated on His throne, high and lifted up. My thought in that moment was, "He is good and He loves me". After my time of reflection, I realized that those words were also the way I would describe my earthly father. It was then I connected the dots. I was limiting God by my earthly experience. I knew both of them were good, and I knew they loved me, but because of the relationship I had with my sweet daddy, who while loving me the best way he knew how, was not able to go to the heart and be intimate and vulnerable. He was a good dad and I always knew that he loved me, but there was a distance I wouldn't have been able to identify until that moment.

Just making this connection between my earthly and Heavenly Father has allowed me to come closer to my Heavenly Father. Jesus has made it possible for me to climb up on the Father's lap, giving me access to His heart. This access makes it safe for me to laugh or cry, to grieve or even question why, while remaining close to the God that created me. This simple revelation has changed not only the way I pray, but it has greatly influenced my experience with God. It has brought heaven to earth.

Now as the workshop approaches, I'm excited to share with others the freedom message of the gospel and to impart biblical principles, exposing the lies we believe and bring us all a little closer to God and to each other. I'm preparing my heart for the quiet that will follow my kiddo's exit. I am realistic about how it will be good and hard all at the same time. Most good things are. But for now, Carli is making dinner and I think I will take that pudgy granddaughter of mine out on the porch to watch papa mow the yard.

ENTRY TWO

I had a really tough conversation with my son this week. We've worked it out, but in a home that is generally peaceful, the conflict between us was very disconcerting. He has been quieter than normal lately and keeping to himself. He has also been expressing frustration with his job, a job that he used to really enjoy. I was hoping to hear what was going on when I invited him out on the porch to touch base. Let's just say it did not go well, at all. He was in no mood to talk, and because he's been so quiet, I did not pick up on his cues, so I initiated a conversation about how he was doing on a day when he was really struggling. You might think wanting to talk on a tough day is a good thing, and for many it may be, but for him on that day, it was especially difficult. As you can imagine, as I said, it did not go well.

So, as I slowly and patiently peppered him with questions, hoping he would open up on his own and connect with me, his annoyance grew, and he did begin to open up angrily, and we eventually got down to the bottom of what's been going on with him. He expressed that living with us, here in our home has been a struggle for him as of late. There's obviously more to it, but this is my book not his, so I will keep it vague to honor him and our relationship.

While our conversation was extremely difficult, when we came back together later to discuss the grievances he expressed, he was the first to apologize and say that he was glad the argument happened, because while it was painful for me, he said upon reflection, it revealed to him just how offended he was and how bitter he had become (my language, not his). I was glad it happened for a different reason. I was just glad to know what was going on with my son, who just a few weeks before appeared to be doing well. I would have preferred a calm conversation, or ideally many conversations, over days to discuss what/how he was feeling, but messy can be good if it gets us to an honest place; however, honest if it is negative has been difficult for us. We've lived keeping the peace much of the time as the culture in our home, and we're not doing that anymore.

Keeping the peace avoids conflict. It avoids disagreements and allows people to wear a mask, requiring true emotions to be stuffed or denied. It appears, or feels like everything is good, when in reality people are struggling. Ideally in relationships, there is a safe give and take of preferences, needs and/or grievances. The quicker and more frequently we kindly communicate them the better, before it turns into bitterness and resentment. In an atmosphere where people are peacemakers, they are real and authentic, which means it may get messy at times. We may have to say a hard word or confront an unhealthy behavior, but messy is a good thing when it means people are getting honest and real.

I don't know why it's so difficult for me to be in conflict with those I love. I suppose most people avoid it, but I'm learning the value of a good disagreement. And now that I'm writing, I'm discovering the issue. We don't always know how to have meaningful, honest, heartfelt conversations. We don't know how to honor while disagreeing. Not at least very well. If we did, we would do it more.

We are learning and growing though, and we are having more meaningful conversations than ever before. I must confess, it still does not come easy for me. I can confront a stranger in the store who is being rude, or even a friend who is overstepping a healthy boundary, but the closest relationships are the hardest for me. To push for accountability and each of us owning our own stuff is a challenge for me. But it's one I'm up for. Since our discussion, my son and I have had a few meetings of the heart. We are in agreement that it is time for him to feel free to be himself in our home. My husband and I have longed for this, but it is easier said than done for our son. And we all agree it's time for him to spread his wings and fly out of the nest. I recognize that this is not a failure on anyone's part. It is a good thing for him and for us. Honestly, it's a little overdue (thank you Covid), which probably added to his frustration.

I spoke the truth in love to Nic, held my ground on how we communicate to one another, and after some time alone, he came back with a tender heart towards his father and I. We don't agree on several things - politics, religion and Jesus, and other things I'm probably not aware of, and that is totally fine with me. We can be in relationship and disagree. One thing I know we are in agreement with, is helping him make a plan to take his next step.

He'll do great no matter where he goes or what he does. I'm so glad we are in relationship while he's making his plans and living his life. I realize that moments like the one we had often end up in estrangement. I'm grateful that did not happen! He's an amazing young man with a sweet tender heart. I'm proud to be his momma. I'm no longer afraid to "go there" with him. Wherever "there" is, because honest and real is the goal. Not disconnection that feels like peace.

ENTRY THREE

Mallory joked the other day that living here was like being on the show *Survivor*. Who will be the last one kicked off the island? While nobody is getting "kicked off", we are approaching the end of a season, and we can all sense the torch being lit. I feel us appreciating our time together as precious once again.

Last night we all hung out. It was so nice for everyone to be here. We watched a movie and played cards together. Nic and Mallory beat Mike and I twice in Euchre. It just wasn't our night. So, I decided to make No Bake Cookies after one of our losses.

I mis-measured the milk four times what the recipe called for. I really wasn't paying attention! Instead of starting over, I decided with a little nudging from Mallory, to increase the rest of the ingredients. If you make No Bakes, you know they are made on the stove and they require just the right amount of slow cooking in order to set up perfectly. After dumping in the rest of the oats and all of the cocoa and several more sticks of butter, I ended up with a gargantuan pot of chocolate yumminess. But it was difficult to judge the boiling time because I was continually adding more ingredients. Needless to say, I ended up with a ridiculous amount of unset chocolate/peanut butter blobs of oatmeal.

I say all of that just to say, I should have cut my loses and started over. It would have taken half the ingredients and they would have turned out with a better consistency, but I felt like I was committed, and I justified the additional effort thinking someone would eat all of these cookies. Probably me.

We did end up with a good laugh while we enjoyed eating the hot cookies with a fork, our favorite way to eat them. But I learned from that silly mistake. Hopefully, I will pay more attention when reading a recipe, and if I do make a big mistake like that again, I will cut my losses and start over. No biggie. Thankfully, this lesson only cost me about ten bucks in groceries. But I think I can apply it to other areas of my life as well.

I once heard a message from Steven Furtick called "God's Will is Whatever". I love this message because it helped me to overcome the fear of being out of God's will. He takes his message from Colossians 3:17, "And whatever you do or say, do it as a representative of the Lord Jesus, giving thanks through Him to God the Father." The point of his message is to not fret and live in fear about the decisions in our lives. If we make a mistake and we are yielded to Him, He is more than capable to make everything work out. Romans 8:28 "We know that God works all things together for our good..." He makes the point that God is way more concerned with who we are rather than with what we do. He can get us where we need to go. When we live with this perspective, we can relax and enjoy life, knowing that we will make mistakes, but if we are willing to course correct quickly when we realize our mistakes, the road on our journey will be much smoother. No more doubling down. No more holding on to people, places and things tightly. Let it go and chalk it up to experience. The quicker, the better.

Cookies are calling

ENTRY FOUR

It's Sunday morning and the sun is finally out. It's been gray and rainy the past four or five days, so the little bit of sunshine through the clouds is a welcome sight. My heart is expectant today as we are all going to church together to celebrate and support Silas getting dedicated to the Lord. What a precious event. When I look at the pictures of him when they moved in last summer I can't believe how much he's grown. When they moved in I don't think he was even crawling, but now he is running around investigating everything. I see so much of my dad, my daughter and my son in him. His big blue eyes, his obedient and sweet heart is so much like all three of them. His daddy is also a gentle, kind, sweet spirit so Silas got a double dose of preciousness. Needless to say, he brings great joy to my heart.

Today, we get to commit to supporting his mom and dad in raising him in the ways of God. The ways of God... what does that even mean? That's a big question, but for me today, it's good to think about what I am committing to. I know the pastor will let us know what we are agreeing to, but this morning, more than anything else, I am resolving to support Mallory and Jacob in loving Silas well. To nurture and communicate with patience and understanding as I interact with him and his parents. I am reminding myself that they are his parents, not me, so I desire to honor them and their choices as they find their path regarding correction, training and parenting styles. Just because my mom did something and I might have done it as well, doesn't mean that is the only way to do it. So, I am reminding myself to stay engaged even when it's not how I would do it. Even more than all of this though, I am committing myself to recognize the reality and power of the Lord God Almighty in the everyday moments of life. The days when we are admiring a sunset, or a flower, or a crying over a skinned knee. I will continue to "let my light shine" with my grandson. To always speak the truth to him in love, and to share the gospel message of

Jesus Christ as we journey on this life together.

What that looks like. Well, I guess we'll figure it out, day by day, as the years turn into decades. As we head off to church, I'm so glad the Spirit of God lives in me and bears witness with my spirit that He is real. I have hope for the future, Silas' future, and our family's future. I know that hard times will continue to come, but I am confident that we are not alone. We have a God that is good, loves us and will always be with us, no matter what.

Hallelujah

JUNE 2021

July

2021
ENTRY ONE

Seasons change, at least in Michigan they do. Even though we are in the middle of Summer, the winds of change are blowing in our house. Boxes are being stored and packed. All of the odd and ends of Carli and Cole's everyday living are being rounded up to once again make the long journey back to Cali. It's been a year already. My how time fly's when you're having fun.

Naturally, this is bittersweet for me. The sweet part is, I love the fact they are moving back to palm trees, beaches and amazing coffee shops, Cole's family and their friends. Both of their hearts are in California, so I'm delighted for them. I also believe it's time for them to spread their wings and fly. I have enjoyed doing life with them so much. With the lockdowns and Covid, we were really thrown together closer than normal, and it really was a precious time. Cooking together, family game nights, movies, bonfires and boat rides, fishing, babies laughing, babies crying and playing, etc. I could go on, but you get the picture. The bitter part is, they will be playing cards and taking walks somewhere else, with someone else.

Next week in the workshop I am leading, we will be discussing the topic of surrender & control. I've been thinking about what it means to surrender, and I can't help but laugh at God's amazing timing. He always is right on time. To surrender... to let go, to trust. If I can surrender my heart again in this season, I can have peace and joy knowing that God is with us all. He will never leave us and He has everything and everyone in His loving care.

I came across this writing I did a few years ago. I called it, "What if?" I feel like it's a great reminder for my heart again today, and hopefully for yours as well.

WHAT IF? →

WHAT IF?

WHAT IF...
TODAY I TRUSTED GOD WITH EVERYTHING. I MEAN EVERYTHING?

WHAT IF...
I BELIEVED DEEP DOWN IN THE CENTER OF MY HEART THAT HE IS GOOD? THAT HE SEES ME AND IS INTIMATELY AWARE OF EVERYTHING I AM GOING THROUGH.

WHAT WOULD HAPPEN IF I DID THAT? WHAT WOULD MY LIFE LOOK LIKE?

WHAT IF...
I BELIEVED THAT WHEN I CALLED ON HIS NAME, HE NOT ONLY HEARS MY PRAYER, BUT IS ACTING ON MY BEHALF?

WHAT IF...
I KEPT MY EYES ON HIM MORE AND ON OTHERS LESS?

WHAT IF...
I JUDGED OTHERS LESS AND LET HIM DEAL WITH THEM?

WHAT IF...
I TRUSTED THAT HE IS JUST, AND WORKING ON MY BEHALF NO MATTER WHAT ANYONE ELSE IS DOING?

WHAT IF...
I LET HIM DEFEND ME AND I WORSHIPED IN THE BATTLE?

WHAT IF...
I UNDERSTOOD THAT HE LOVES MY PEOPLE EVEN MORE THAN I DO?

WHAT IF...
I RESPECT THEM ENOUGH TO LET THEM CHOOSE FOR THEMSELVES?

WHAT IF...
I RESPECTED THEM LIKE HE DOES?

WHAT IF...
I LOVE THEM AND LET GOD FIX THEM?

WHAT IF...
HE'S WANTING TO WORK IN THEIR HEART AND LIFE, AND I'M GETTING IN THE WAY?

WHAT IF...
HARDSHIP AND/OR PAIN IS THE VERY THING THEY NEED TO BRING THEM TO THE END OF THEMSELVES, MOTIVATING THEM TO CALL OUT TO GOD... AND I MET THE NEED INSTEAD?

WHAT IF...
I AM GETTING IN THE WAY INSTEAD OF HELPING?

WHAT IF...

I TRUSTED GOD? WHAT IF I BELIEVED HIS WORD? ALL OF IT?

WHAT IF…
I TRUSTED MY MARRIAGE, MY CHILDREN AND THEIR FUTURES, MY FINANCES, MY MINISTRY AND MY DAY TO THE LORD.

WHAT IF…
I UNDERSTOOD THAT I HAVE A CHOICE? THAT WHILE HE HAS A FUTURE AND A HOPE FOR ME, I'VE STILL GOT TO DO SOMETHING?

WHAT IF…
I STOPPED WAITING AND STARTED BELIEVING IN FAITH FOR SOMETHING.

WHAT IF…
I TOOK A RISK AND BELIEVED THAT HE WILL CATCH ME IF I FALL?

WHAT IF I TRUSTED THAT HE COULD LEAD ME BY HIS HOLY SPIRIT THAT LIVES INSIDE OF ME?

WHAT IF…
I AM ABLE TO HEAR HIS STILL SMALL VOICE AND OBEY. WHAT WOULD HAPPEN IF I DID THAT? WHAT COULD HE DO THROUGH ME?

WHAT IF…
I LOOKED TO HEAVEN AND HELD MY HANDS WIDE OPEN AND SAID, "HAVE YOUR WAY LORD JESUS!"?

JULY 2021

WHAT IF...
I SAID, "I SURRENDER, I TRUST YOU"?

——————— **ENTRY** ———————
TWO

Picture this, Mel Gibson yelling "They'll never take away — OUR FREEDOM!" From the movie *Braveheart*. I hate the fighting in that movie, but I love the themes. Freedom, loyalty, honor, love, brotherhood, etc. Today is the Fourth of July, and I continue to be so grateful for the freedoms we have living in America. It may not look like it used to, but it is still an amazing country. The best country in the world in my opinion, and I'm grateful to live here.

The sun is shining, thank the Lord, and it's the kind of day you hope to have living on the lake. The lemonade is chilling, so is the potato and fruit salad. We are keeping it small this year. With everything that has been going on, we are all a little tired. I'm looking forward to sitting on the porch and watching the littles play in the sprinkler and kiddie pool. Hot dogs are on the menu, keeping the prep simple and the cook time quick. I know my limits, so this day is about enjoying family and a few friends, and remembering the sacrifices that men and women have made to make this relaxing day possible for us.

As I ponder the concept of freedom, I'm reminded of love. How there is no control or fear in "true" love. The freedom to choose that God has granted us amazes me. When choice is taken away, love is no longer love. It becomes slavery, manipulation, bondage. For example, I live with my husband in our home. We are both free to come and go as we please. We have both chosen to be dedicated to one another, committed to our relationship. But what if one day Mike took me to the basement and chained me to the pipe in the storage room and left me there. What we have would no longer be love, it would become slavery. Same people, same house, the only thing that has changed is free will. I no longer have the choice, therefore it is no longer love.

Our Heavenly Father doesn't want slaves tied up so they have to be with Him. He desires that all would come to know Him. That's why Jesus came. That's the beauty and the rub. The choice He has given us, to believe in Jesus as our Lord and Savior, or not to. We all get to choose this day who we will serve. We get to choose how we will live our lives. When Jesus encountered the rich young ruler in Matthew 19, He didn't beg the young man to follow Him. He didn't lecture Him about what will happen to him if he doesn't desire Jesus over his riches. He tells him the truth and lets him decide for himself. Free will in action. I don't know about you, but I have not respected people enough to let them choose on their own, not without a heavy dose of convincing from me. I can imagine if I were there, I would have chased after the young man and explained further the consequences of his walking away. I would have implored him to sell his belongings because I know they will never satisfy like a relationship with Jesus. But Jesus never manipulates or begs. He reveals truths and values choice.

Another example of the beauty of freedom is found in the story of the prodigal son found in Luke 15. There is so much beauty in this story, I could write a whole book on it. For today my takeaway is, the youngest son didn't want to live with his father or his family any longer. He wanted his money so he could live for himself and do what he wanted to do. At this request, his father didn't lecture him. He didn't shame him. He didn't give him the silent treatment in an effort to change his mind. The father knew the power of experience, so he gave his son what he asked for and let him walk away. No lecture. No argument. Wow! He's not angry, and we know this because he is waiting for his son to come home. Allowing him to choose and hopefully realize the error of his ways, to experience repentance or whatever life holds for him living with only himself in mind. He is waiting with open arms to take him back. To lovingly accept him. This shows not only the beauty of our Heavenly Father's heart, but it reveals how much He values freedom. Freedom to choose Him and His ways, and the freedom to walk in the opposite direction if we want to.

I love my husband. I love that every day I get to say, "I choose you". After thirty five years of marriage, isn't that a beautiful thing? I treasure the fact that he says it to me as well every day. Not always with words, but so often with the choices he makes. Valuing communication, calling when he will be late or just to ask how my day is going. Valuing our home by planting flowers he knows I love and maintaining what we have. Valuing himself by making healthy choices, taking care of his soul health and his possessions. The freedom we give each other to be ourselves and to grow and change is what I love about our marriage. It's also what I love about my relationship with God. His grace for my life, and His unending desire for me to run to him with everything. He is always waiting for me with a ring for my hand, a robe for my back and shoes for my tired feet. It's a beautiful thing. This thing called...

JULY 2021

ENTRY THREE

And then there were six. Carli, Cole and little Ms. Stevie left for California this week. It is definitely bitter sweet. I am happy for them to move on and to experience new things together as a married couple. It's as it should be, but that doesn't mean my heart isn't aching and missing them every single day. Thankfully for me, Carli makes these amazing little videos on Instagram documenting their lives, so we are able to get a look at their hotels, their food excursions and to watch them on the road along the way. And, I get to see Stevie's face and hear her little voice. It makes my heart so happy.

They really lived with us. We shared the same kitchen, living room and yard. We were together all of the time, sharing meals and chores and music. They did not have the luxury of the privacy of the basement apartment, and they handled it with amazing grace. I give Cole a lot of credit. He experienced his first year as a husband and then as a father, living with his in-laws, and even though we are amazing, wink wink, it could not have been easy. We did part on great terms. I'm so grateful for that. We can honestly say that we love each other more, and even like each other more, after our yearlong experiment on the lake.

When we finally got everything packed in their vehicle and closed the door, barely, on the U-Haul, we all sat down exhausted in the living room and took a look back at our time together. We laughed about some of the things that happened during the year, and we teared up at some of the difficult and tender moments we experienced together. What a beautiful memory. It is a gift I will cherish for the rest of my life.

We don't know what the future holds for any of us. We are all in the Lord's hands. Loving life and listening to His voice. I am hoping that we will live near each other again someday. I hope we will have Sunday dinners together and I will be able to babysit my grandkids often. If I don't, I know we will always find a way to each other. We will connect often, and we will always have the memories of the year on the lake.

Sniffle.

JULY 2021

August

2021
ENTRY ONE

Blindness runs in my family, or so it did. I'm taking a stand here and now to declare healing for myself and for our future generations. It has been said, "Our people" on my mom's side can't see. They have lived with cataracts, glaucoma and/or macular degeneration for generations. My mom's grandma went blind and her dad had his cataract-affected lenses taken out when he was in his fifties. He wore pop bottle glasses to replace them for the rest of his life.

My sweet momma has had cataract surgery already and has been living with Macular Degeneration for years. This means she is living life only seeing a fraction of her reality. It's been progressive and has slowly made it very difficult for her to see anything with any detail. She can see people, but can't tell who they are until she hears a voice or is able to be around them long enough to put the puzzle pieces together, identifying who they are. Their voice, their hair, clothing style, height, etc. She is able to put the pieces together quickly, but the center of her vision is black, so it's always a guessing game. She, like her father, is coping well. She manages living alone at home very well for the time being. Along with her vision, she has lost her independence. Selling her car was traumatic for her. No longer having the ability to say when and where she wanted to go has been very difficult for such a strong independent woman.

I can relate to her situation more than I would like. I am currently dealing with my own cataract struggle. I've already had surgery on my left eye, and I'm so grateful that the technology is so much better now than it was when my grandpa needed it. I have a new, clear lens replacing my old one. No need for glasses or contacts in that eye. It's actually better than the original lens was before the cataract as I've had to wear contacts every day of my adult life, but with the new lens, I see better than ever. I sure do wish my grandpa could have experienced the miracles of modern medicine like I have.

However, my right eye is virtually blind from a cataract. It has deteriorated quickly. Light bothers me and I can't read anything up close without cheaters, and even then it's tough to see. To say it's very uncomfortable, is an understatement. In a few weeks I will have surgery on my right eye, hopefully making it better than it has ever been. Every day until then, I will look through this cloudy, unfocused lens. This temporary blindness is imparting the gift of ever increasing compassion and empathy for my mother.

Empathy, the ability to understand and share the feelings of another. What a gift. I am praying and believing that blindness stops here, with my mother and I. Fortunately, I have no signs of glaucoma or Macular Degeneration. I truly believe it will stay that way. I am also believing that for my children and grandchildren as well. I am however, taking note of what this experience is like. The headaches, the discomfort from the light, the inability to read simple instructions without having my glasses available. All of this inconvenience is temporary for me, so I really can't complain. Moving forward, what I can do is be patient and kind when I want to get frustrated with my mother. I can make an effort to visit more even though I know she has many visitors and is loved well by our family, her neighbors and friends. I can live from this renewed sense of empathy and never forget the days when it was difficult to see and I had to ask for help.

Never forget

AUGUST 2021

ENTRY TWO

"Trust in the Lord with all of your heart, and lean not on your own understanding. In all of your ways acknowledge Him, and He will direct your steps." Proverbs 3:5 "When I am afraid, I put my trust in You" Psalm 56:3, and one more just for fun from Jeremiah 17:7, "Blessed is the person who trusts in the Lord, whose confidence is in Him." Here I am again. Helpless to change a situation that directly impacts my life.

Several times Mike and I have felt led to take risks with regards to his business, and while we have always had faith and peace, many of his business adventures have not turned out quite like we hoped they would. Mike sells pharmaceuticals and not long after we moved into this house on the lake, he stepped out in faith once again and joined a company that had a very promising drug that was almost ready to head to market. We found out this week that the FDA has denied their request for approval. At least it looks as though that will be their decision because they didn't have sufficient evidence that the drug would be effective, or something like that. We will get the final word next week, but if that is indeed the case again, Mike will be looking for another job. The last time this happened, he was out of work for thirteen months and as you can imagine, that was not fun, at all. This time he will be fifty-nine. In all honesty his age is adding to the anxiety, but I can honestly say, I am not afraid. I know this man's reputation and the relationships he has established throughout his amazing career. And, I know that God brought us to this place, so He will not leave us here alone.

I must admit, God did some amazing things in both of our hearts during the last season of unemployment. He also did some amazing things in our relationship as well. You really find out what is inside of you when you get squeezed good and tight. We were pleasantly surprised that what came out of us was faith, hope and love.

So, I can honestly say I am not afraid. I know that we heard God's voice to take this specific job, so I am praying and excited to see what God is going to do. I'm praying for a miracle and asking God for favor with the FDA. Wouldn't that be amazing? If for some reason that does not happen and it is the Lord's will for Mike to work for another company selling another drug, we will be okay. After knowing Jesus for this long and trusting Him with our lives over and over again, I am confident He's got us. Who knows, maybe there will be a career change, or another move in our future. Who knows? God does! One thing I am sure of is that my God sees me and knows me and loves me. I have years of experience to pull from to remind my heart of this truth.

So, here we go again. Trusting in the Lord with all of our hearts. For our livelihood. For our children and their children. For all of it. It sure beats worrying and fretting. I'm reminded as I write, of the scripture the Lord gave me as a promise and a praise in the first of the year.

"My heart is confident in You, O God; my heart is confident. No wonder I can sing Your praises! Wake up, my heart! Wake up, O lyre and harp. I will wake the dawn with my song. I will thank you, Lord, among all the people. I will sing Your praises among the nations. For Your unfailing love is as high as the heavens. Your faithfulness reaches to the clouds. Be exalted, O God, above the highest heavens. May Your glory shine over all the earth." Psalm 57:7

ENTRY THREE

Teamwork makes the dream work. We had a very busy weekend and the crazy is continuing throughout this week. Today, we are finally getting a little concrete driveway, sidewalk, basketball court, and a patio for the side of our house. It's been a long time coming. When we bought the house there was no landscaping and nothing was finished. Last summer not many companies were up and running, and this summer they are all slammed because of the shutdowns. I'm unusually happy to be getting this work done. Because I'm so happy, I've been sitting on my front porch gawking at the workers, wait, that doesn't sound right! I've been admiring how they all work together so well. Whew! Seriously though, they are taking an area of dirt and ratty grass and sculpting it with this structured chaos. Rocks and mud get poured and everyone gets to work. Before you know it, there is a smooth, finished sidewalk.

There is a team of about ten guys working at our house, and everyone has a job. They are each responsible for something that is necessary but not noticeably important, but each action builds on the former one to complete the job. It's like a dance. One pours the rocky sludge into just the right area from his ginormous truck. You can tell this guy does this every day. It's the precise amount in exactly the correct spot. Then the men get to work moving it all into place. One guy lifts the grate so the concrete has strength in the middle. Another pushes it all around, filling in all of the gaps. Several begin to smooth it out with a piece of wood, and then there's the finesse guy. He's already starting to smooth it out at the corner and moving towards the center with another tool. It looks like he's frosting a really big cake. He takes the chunky, messy mixture and turns it into a beautiful platform to walk, drive and play on.

As I watched them all step into action, working together, anticipating each others' moves and needs, I was reminded of this past weekend. Mike and I volunteered at the Barn where I teach and council. We helped host a worship night and then the next day a baptismal service for the precious people whose lives have been changed this year by Jesus and the ministry of Barn 45. We were also part of a team, working together, anticipating each others' needs. I had the privilege of greeting everyone with a name tag. People came from all over Michigan and the country. They wrote their name and where they were coming from, so I got to see the locations they traveled from and hear some of their stories. Two lovely ladies who Zoom in on my class came from out of state. One from Seattle, Washington and the other from southern Ohio. It was incredible to hug their necks and see their faces without the Brady Bunch square around their heads that only Zoom can provide. Others came from Florida, New York, California, New Jersey and all over the state of Michigan.

Thank you Covid, for closing everything down so that Joy and Tara could discuss the Word of God every morning on Facebook Live and reach thousands of people instead of hundreds. What the devil meant for harm, God uses for good. These precious people from all over the state and country, and actually the world, would never have had the opportunity to be a part of this unique Bible study if it weren't for the struggle caused by the lockdowns.

I think of those who set it all up, those of us who worked while the events were happening and those of us that cleaned up. We were moving and working together like this crew in my yard today. We are all exhausted, but our hearts are full. Some plant, some water and some reap the harvest. I loved getting to watch it all.

Time for some hopscotch

ENTRY FOUR

My heart is heavy today. Very heavy. In the past month, four people that I know, some for 20+ years, have passed away. Two of them have been fighting illness' for years and just recently lost their battles. The others have been relatively sudden and random. One after another, I got the news to pray. "They've taken a sudden turn for the worst. It's bad, pray." Or, I see on Facebook or I get a text that another precious soul is gone. Just gone. They were seemingly healthy last week, and they are gone to be with the Lord this week. I cannot recall another time in my life when so many people that I know have passed away in such a short amount of time. It's very odd, and a little unnerving.

I'm wrestling today with God's sovereignty and loving grace, and my inability to understand the kingdom of God fully. We see through a glass dimly... I'm feelin' it today. I was tempted to sit down to write this morning before I spent time with Jesus. I just wanted to get it all out, but I knew better. I know to seek the kingdom first. To place my heart again in the Father's loving hands before I go to anything or anyone in this world to make me feel better or to find answers. So, I got it all out in prayer and quiet reflection. To be honest, as I write, I can admit, I didn't get any great revelations, but I did experience the peace of His presence. My daily reading was in James where I've been for the past couple of days. Today's caption in James 5 was "The power of prayer". As I read it, I chuckled. Of course that's today's reading. As I continued on, "Are any of you suffering hardships?" I cried out, "Yes!" So many people I know are dealing with the pain and heartache of illness, marriage's on the brink and the stresses of life and of death. My heart aches for them and I've been praying for some of them for years. Then, James 5:14 went on to ask, "Are any of you sick?" "Yes!" Cancer, mental illness, blindness. My sweet grandbaby Stevie is living with severe eczema and allergies. We've been praying and believing that the Spirit of God, the power that raised Jesus from the dead, would touch these lives and bring healing and life to these dear ones. James goes on to tell us that prayer offered in faith will heal the sick and the Lord will make them well. I believe this or I wouldn't keep praying! I have seen miracles happen.

We were told by a Fertility Specialist at The Cleveland Clinic thirty-five years ago, "You better believe in miracles because there is no way you're ever going to get pregnant". We looked at each other and said emphatically, "We do"!

We prayed and then continued to pray. Our people prayed and continued to pray and after years of trying we finally got our miracle. Then we got two more.

God has provided for my husband and myself. He has lead us and directed our steps. He has protected us and our children. When I have called to Him, He has answered me. I know this. I trust this in my life. What do I do today as I carry this heaviness in my chest, knowing that another precious man in his fifties, that we've been praying for, passed away last night after a several week battle with Covid? I pause, I wait, and I breathe. I look out at the water with its thousands of light diamonds shining in the sunlight. I feel the breeze coming in through the window beside me and I melt into the sound of the gentle playlist seeping from my speaker. I rest in Jonathan Ogden's lyrics to his song, *With You*, "when I consider the heavens, and the works of your fingers and all of the stars that You have made, who am I that you are thinking of me? Oh, I just want to be with you, I just want to be with you." It's the cry of my heart today. I don't have the answers to the "why" questions bumping up against each other in my head. I only know that I need the Spirit of God to comfort me. I just need to be with my Jesus for a while.

I believe in the power of prayer. I believe what the Word of God says about prayer all throughout the Word. I see the examples of Esther and David, Hannah and Isaiah, Timothy, James and Paul, and so many more, not to mention the example Jesus sets for us to pray. He got alone to pray often. If He needed to pray, to pour out His heart to His Father in times of need. To be with Him and get guidance and direction, how much more do I need to? If He trusted Him, so can I. One of His final prayers comes to mind as I write, "Not my will, but Yours be done". As I complete today's writing, I will rest my heart and mind there. I know I don't see the bigger picture. I know this world is not my home. I believe that all of the people who have left us are with the Lord right now. This is my hope, and it helps to know that I will see them again one day. I will posture myself to rest in this truth today.

I will take a deep breath and then I will do it again. I will thank Him for the beauty of this day, even though I don't always understand. I will trust Him with all of my heart, knowing if I lean on my own understanding I will sink down deep in the waves of confusion and despair. I choose to take my cue from Jesus today, and not what the world tells me.

I'm sad today and it's okay

ENTRY FIVE

What a difference a day makes. Today is a new day. I feel refreshed body — mind and spirit. It doesn't hurt that I got a massage this morning, but this refreshing is so much deeper than physical. Last night my sweet hubby invited me on to our boat to watch the sunset together. I declined as I didn't have the energy and wanted to veg in front of the TV, so I continued to make myself a salad. Then, he nudged me again to join him, so I reluctantly took my salad out on the boat and we sat in the stillness of the water. His instrumental worship playlist merging with the songs of the crickets and occasional birds songs began to feed my soul. He fished and I sat in the stillness of the sunset. The bright orange sun had a clear path to the horizon as the clouds had blown north, just enough for us to enjoy the show.

AUGUST 2021

Draping from one of the distant clouds was a stream of rain that was cool to watch from a distance, but I was hoping wouldn't steal our evening. Upon questioning Mike about this, he shrugged and said, "I've seen The Notebook". I guess he wasn't worried about getting wet, so I wasn't either.

The idea of getting caught in the rain and making the mental decision in my mind that we would still be alright, even if we got drenched, was a moment of letting go for me. We'd be okay. Maybe it would be even more memorable and fun if we did get swept away in a summer shower. It's okay if we get wet. It's okay if it doesn't look like I thought it would. This evening gently ushered in a sweet conversation about all that has been going on in our lives. The deaths we are processing. The turmoil in Afghanistan this week. The earthquake and hurricane in Haiti and our preparing for our son's departure. It all got blended in hot tears running down my face. It was a shower alright, just not coming from the sky.

As I look back on yesterday's grief and the trials that so many of us are processing, I continue to ache for all of the people living intimately with the above mentioned events. They are heavy and painful to ponder, but I have peace today in the midst of the struggle. My friend Joy went on Facebook Live yesterday. I watched her short video admonishment in the afternoon and was so grateful for her added perspective, as she too has been experiencing a lot lately. It partnered with what I wrote so well. She was encouraging those who are feeling the weight of this world to pray. She cited Philippians 4:6-7, "Don't worry about anything; instead, pray about everything. Tell God what you need, and thank Him for all that He has done. Then you will experience God's peace, which exceeds anything we can understand. His peace will guard your hearts and minds as you live in Christ Jesus." This peace. This wonderful peace that can envelope us in the midst of the storm. What a wonderful gift.

Nothing has really changed from yesterday to today, but taking it all to the Lord in prayer each day, spending time in nature and in precious conversation was the perfect prescription for my heartache. I am grateful for the voices in my life that always bring me back to center, to the truth. God's Word and His gentle whisper in my heart. A relationship with the Almighty God, who is always listening and attentive to my plea. Faithful and Spirit-led relationships that listen, encourage and can be trusted. These are the ingredients that hold me up when I feel weak. They are the foundation that holds my course steady, though the wind may blow... hard.

Lookin'for a rainbow

AUGUST 2021

ENTRY SIX

The leaves are just barely beginning to change color and fall from the trees. I see little glimpses of red and yellow as I drive down our country road. Most of the canopy that covers the dirt roads leading to our house on the lake are still green, but the wind is beginning to blow and I am very aware that fall is just around the corner.

This week I am making plans to travel with Nic to California, as he is going to venture off on his own near his sissy and Cole's family. He has been making plans to head west for a while now, and the time has come for us to say "Good-bye for now". He is heading out next week, and my offer to road trip with him was surprisingly and joyfully met with great reception. I am looking forward to this special time traveling across America with my son, and I can't wait to visit with Carli, Cole, Stevie and Cole's family, and then set him up in the room he will be renting. Looks like Mallory, Jacob and Sy are the "last ones on the island" after all.

Approximately five years ago, Mike made the exact same trip with Carli when she moved to California to make her own way in the world. She was the same age as Nic is now. Mike and Carli had a great time traveling and exploring together, and none of us could have known then what the future would hold for all of us this past year.

Who knows what the next five years will hold? As I write this last entry I am at rest and full of hope and peace for the future. No one knows what the days ahead hold for any of us, but we do know Who holds the future. That is one thing I am sure of. As this season comes to an end, I am aware that this is where my book must end. We will go on to have babies/grandbabies, throw parties, cry through struggles, and have many more stories, as that's life. I will miss being able to share the journey with you, my invisible companions who were along for the ride.

This past year has been one for the record books. Literally. So many bizarre and unique events in the world and in our lives. Generational living through Covid shutdowns, tumultuous elections, unrest in our cities, tragic earthquakes and hurricanes all around the world, births, deaths, and all of the everyday life that fills in the gaps.

It has been my joy to share our little piece of the puzzle with you. I hope that you have enjoyed the journey as well. I hope you laughed and cried alongside me, and found some camaraderie in your own life situations. More than anything, I hope my words have always directed you to the only One who can satisfy and change your life – Jesus.

As I end this writing journey, I am aware that I do not have a profound ending to our story. There was not a worldwide event other than the above mentioned, requiring us to all live together for a year. Just ordinary lives continuing to live this extraordinary life we are given. I am guessing that the future will gently and slowly reveal what the Lord was up to by bringing us together for this special time on the lake. Relationships were deepened, I am sure of that. My euchre game has improved, I'm pretty sure of that as well. I've got at least twenty pounds to lose from all of the yummy meals we've enjoyed together, and my heart is overflowing with all of the memories we have made living life together, and I do mean together. You can't get what we've gained over the phone, or through FaceTime. While technological advances are great and they do bring us closer, there's nothing quite like waking up in the middle of the night to creepy talking smoke detectors, heart pounding, hair tousled, exploring the house for the potential fire. And you can't smell the popcorn setting on the table while we all play a game together on a Saturday night over a text, and I wouldn't trade being in the room while Stevie pushed her way into the world for anything. I've cherished seeing my little Silas almost every single day, at the very least for a smooch or snack, for over a year. And now I am getting to watch Silas' little brother move like a gymnast inside Mallory's tummy, impatiently waiting to make his grand entrance. I've loved all of it. I treasure every moment. The conversations, the tears, the dinners together, the bonfires, the dishes... Well, I don't miss the dishes. But the deep workings of God in our lives during our time together is yet to be revealed.

So here, in my modest conclusion, I leave you with this inspiring quote from the movie Love Story. "Loving means never having to say you're sorry". No wait! That is possibly the worst line in movie history. Say you're sorry, and do it often. That is for sure one of the things I've learned from this past year. Being "quick to listen, slow to speak and slow to become angry" as stated in James 1:19 is really good advice. No matter who you live with.

The quote I really want to leave you with is one of my favorites from General Maximus Decimus Meridius in the movie *Gladiator*.

"What we do in life, echoes in eternity."

The End

COME TO Jesus

God loves you. He has an amazing plan for your life. If you do not have a personal relationship with Jesus Christ, you can.

The Bible tells us how forgiveness and relationship with God are possible...

John 3:16 says, "For God so loved the world so much that He gave His one and only Son, so that everyone who believes in Him will not perish but have eternal life."

Romans 3:22-25 tell us, "We are made right with God by placing our faith in Jesus Christ. And this is true for everyone who believes, no matter who we are. For everyone has sinned; we all fall short of God's glorious standard. Yet God, with underserved kindness, declares that we are righteous. He did this through Christ Jesus when He freed us from the penalty for our sins. God presented Jesus as the sacrifice for sin. People are made right with God when they believe that Jesus sacrificed His life, shedding His blood."

Romans 10:9-10 says, "If you confess with your mouth that Jesus is Lord and believe in your heart that God raised Him from the dead, you will be saved. For it is by believing in your heart that you are made right with God, and it is by confessing with your mouth that you are saved."

If you want to give your heart/life to God, it's as simple as inviting Him in.

Here is a sample Salvation Prayer to get you started. You can't do it wrong, prayer is just a conversation between you and God. Your words are sweet to His heart.

Jesus, I believe you are Lord. I believe you died and were raised to life so that I might be forgiven and have relationship with God. I give you my life and I trust that You will show me what that looks like. Thank you for forgiving and loving me. I receive it.

In Jesus name,

Amen

I PRAY THAT FROM HIS GLORIOUS, UNLIMITED RESOURCES HE WILL EMPOWER YOU WITH INNER STRENGTH THROUGH HIS SPIRIT. 17 THEN CHRIST WILL MAKE HIS HOME IN YOUR HEARTS AS YOU TRUST IN HIM. YOUR ROOTS WILL GROW DOWN INTO GOD'S LOVE AND KEEP YOU STRONG. 18 AND MAY YOU HAVE THE POWER TO UNDERSTAND, AS ALL GOD'S PEOPLE SHOULD, HOW WIDE, HOW LONG, HOW HIGH, AND HOW DEEP HIS LOVE IS. 19 MAY YOU EXPERIENCE THE LOVE OF CHRIST, THOUGH IT IS TOO GREAT TO UNDERSTAND FULLY. THEN YOU WILL BE MADE COMPLETE WITH ALL THE FULLNESS OF LIFE AND POWER THAT COMES FROM GOD.

20 NOW ALL GLORY TO GOD, WHO IS ABLE, THROUGH HIS MIGHTY POWER AT WORK WITHIN US, TO ACCOMPLISH INFINITELY MORE THAN WE MIGHT ASK OR THINK. 21 GLORY TO HIM IN THE CHURCH AND IN CHRIST JESUS THROUGH ALL GENERATIONS FOREVER AND EVER! AMEN.

EPHESIANS 3:16-21

Announcing

BRADY MICHAEL INGRAM

SEPTEMBER 20, 2021

ABOUT THE AUTHOR

Teri has always had a zeal for writing, and now in her fifties, is publishing her second book *Time Well Spent,* following *Death of a Church Lady* (available at terimillerministries.com - not available on Amazon).

In addition to writing, she is a Licensed Biblical Counselor and member of the National Christian Counselors Association. As a counselor, she is passionate about building strong relationships with people, helping them to personally hear God's voice and apply the Truth found in the Word of God in ways that are meaningful, healing, and life-giving.

Teri leads The Healed & Set Free Workshop at Barn 45. This life-changing teaching deals with Codependency, Shame, Identity, Family Systems, Love, Boundaries and much more. Teri greatly enjoys the opportunities she is presented with to share with others what God has done in her life.

On warm summer mornings you can find Teri on the back porch, Bible in hand, sipping her morning coffee. She has been married to her handsome hubby, Michael, for thirty-five years and is blessed with three grown children, two sons-in-law and three amazing grandbabies.

TERIMILLERMINISTRIES.COM